PRACTICAL S

D1628161

Series Editor

BASW

Editorial Advisory Board:
Robert Adams, Terry Bamford, Charles Barker,
Lena Dominelli, Malcolm Payne, Michael Preston-Shoot,
Daphne Statham and Jane Tunstill

Social work is at an important stage in its development. All professions must be responsive to changing social and economic conditions if they are to meet the needs of those they serve. This series focuses on sound practice and the specific contributions which social workers can make to the well-being of our society.

The British Association of Social Workers has always been conscious of its role in setting guidelines for practice and in seeking to raise professional standards. The concept of the Practical Social Work series arose from a survey of BASW members to discover where they, the practitioners in social work, felt there was the most need for new literature. The response was overwhelming and enthusiastic, and the result is a carefully planned, coherent series of books. The emphasis is firmly on practice set in a theoretical framework. The books will inform, stimulate and promote discussion, thus adding to the further development of skills and high professional standards. All the authors are practitioners and teachers of social work, representing a wide variety of experience.

JO CAMPLING

A list of published titles in this series follows overleaf

Practical Social Work
Series Standing Order ISBN 0–333–69347–7
(*outside North America only*)

You can receive future titles in this series as they are published by placing a standing order. Please contact your bookseller or, in the case of difficulty, write to us at the address below with your name and address, the title of the series and the ISBN quoted above.

Customer Services Department, Macmillan Distribution Ltd
Houndmills, Basingstoke, Hampshire RG21 6XS, England

PRACTICAL SOCIAL WORK

Effective Groupwork

Michael Preston-Shoot

Published by
MACMILLAN PRESS LTD
Houndmills, Basingstoke, Hampshire RG21 6XS
and London
Companies and representatives
throughout the world

ISBN 0–333–40987–6 hardcover
ISBN 0–333–40988–4 paperback

This book is printed on paper suitable for recycling and
made from fully managed and sustained forest sources.

A catalogue record for this book is available
from the British Library.

Transferred to digital printing, 2002

Printed and bound in Great Britain by
Antony Rowe Ltd, Chippenham and Eastbourne

Contents

Preface

I could not have written this book without the encouragement, enthusiasm and valuable guidance of many friends and colleagues. My thanks especially to Professor Dorothy Whitaker and Lesley Archer at the University of York for guiding me through my research into co-leadership in groupwork and for commenting on the first draft of the book; to Tim Cook, formerly Director of Family Service Units, and Janet Williams at National Office, Family Service Units; to all my colleagues in Family Service Units and to participants on the groupwork workshops I have led, whose willingness to share their ideas and practice experiences have helped to shape my book; to Vera Rainforth and Rosanna Whitehead for their help in typing the text.

I dedicate my book to Eva Seligman with whom I found my creativity and the release to express it.

MICHAEL PRESTON-SHOOT

Introduction

Groupwork occupies a variable position within social work. For some practitioners it represents a method of working effectively with a wide range of client groups and symbolises a new approach to demands which overburden social work teams. Its use may reflect a search for an economic use of resources or an antidote to doubts about the effectiveness of casework. Its attractiveness may lie also in the value position it can enhance, namely the conviction that people can be understood and helped only when they are considered alongside the systems and networks in which they function. Thus groupwork may be seen as enhancing the movement away from seeing clients as the passive recipients of services and as people with needs. For other practitioners, however, groupwork remains a peripheral or extra-curricula activity on the fringe of social work, something difficult to incorporate into overstretched workloads or to integrate with the traditional approach to the organisation of social work services.

Some of the reasons for this variable position are structural. More often than not, groupwork is another demanding responsibility placed on top of an already substantial workload and undertaken without supervision. It requires, therefore, a high degree of commitment and enthusiasm for any practitioner to offer to do it and to establish a continuity of experience which allows the development of skills and knowledge as groupworkers. Equally unhelpful is the brief acknowledgement given to groupwork in some qualifying courses and in-service training. Consequently, it is not

1

surprising that practitioners feel ill-equipped for the task (Davies, 1984). Another organisational obstacle lies in the interaction between workers and their agency. Practitioners may feel that to practise professionally requires clarity and specificity concerning the aims of the proposed group and the formulation of a proposal according to the assessment of the workers. However, to obtain acceptance of the proposal to lead a group and to enlist the co-operation of colleagues, practitioners may feel constrained to devise a group which is acceptable to their agency and to refrain from being too specific.

The term groupwork complicates the situation further since it is an all-encompassing description of activities which vary from group therapy and social groupwork to social action, self-help and consciousness-raising. Some groups are problem-centred, others are not. The intention may be to alleviate social isolation, to prepare people for new experiences, to resolve or prevent problems, or to provide some form of learning opportunity. There are a variety of theoretical frameworks and leadership styles so that it can be difficult to identify which knowledge-base is the most appropriate. Some approaches emphasise individual-centred aims and focus on the needs and reactions of individuals. Others stress the importance of group-centred aims or social change goals. These groups may concentrate on attempting to change social attitudes towards group members or to tap members' capabilities which are overshadowed in traditional social work methods which emphasise individual needs. The result is that groupwork can appear a daunting enterprise.

Research has found that practitioners are concerned about their need for support and their lack of confidence, and anxious about what they perceive to be their limited skills and competence. Intending groupworkers are often ambivalent, even fearful about groups, concerned about a group's potential for destructiveness. Other common fears are that they will lose control of the group, encounter unmanageable situations or be unable to contain attacks on the leaders within the group. Various other practice-related questions also confront practitioners wishing to explore this method of working. The following have been met:

- which clients might benefit from which types of groups?
- how might the group be presented to potential members so as to engage them?
- how should members be selected and the length of the group determined?
- what guidelines are available on forming a group?
- what should be the group's focus and how may groupwork become an economical use of resources?
- how can groupworkers include all the group's members and keep to the format of the group?
- how might groupworkers enable a group to become self-supporting and hand back the leadership role to members?

This book aims to set out the basic issues and to attempt some answers; it aims also to enhance the reader's awareness of the issues and sense of the feasibility of groupwork in two ways. First, to provide a practice guide for social workers either involved or interested in groupwork. With its emphasis on promoting skills in the preparation and leadership of groups, on what facilitates effective planning, leadership and evaluation of groupwork, this book aims to equip groupworkers with a structure for practice and to bring some sense to a complex process. Thus, each chapter will outline key practice issues and offer some guidelines. There will be no differentiation between social work settings, types of groups or client groups since the skills and tasks involved are substantially the same and the framework applicable whatever the setting or type of group envisaged. Rather, the stages and processes of groupwork will be described.

Secondly, to consider co-working alongside single leadership. Co-leadership, the presence of two or more practitioners working together in a group, is the prevalent modality in groupwork practice, enjoying widespread use across different types of groups and settings (Brown *et al.*, 1982). However, it has received a rather uncritical and unstudied embrace. Much of the literature continues to assume single leaders or discusses the phenomenon of co-work briefly. Descriptive accounts of groupwork rarely contain comments on co-leadership and even less frequently consider in depth this method of working. This trend is surprising and disappointing since co-work is exceedingly complex and personally demanding.

Accordingly, many practice-related questions occur, particularly:

- what are the factors which should be considered in the selection of co-workers?
- in what circumstances is co-leadership necessary and effective?
- what types of groups benefit from the presence of more than one worker?
- what factors contribute to a successful working relationship between co-workers?
- what is the impact of the group on the co-workers and their impact as a partnership on the group?
- what is the relative efficacy of co-leadership as against single leadership?
- what should be the weighting given to the preferences of groupworkers, agency norms, the needs of the groups, client wishes and client needs in the selection of the leadership modality?

This book attempts to answer some of these questions and to give detailed consideration to co-working within groupwork. It is not written on the assumption of single leaders, rather the reverse. Where the discussion applies to single and co-leaders alike, the co-work terminology will be used to reflect this modality's widespread prevalence. Solo and co-leadership will be compared, examined and contrasted throughout and a structure for practice within which this choice is one component will be provided.

Two beliefs underpin this aspect of the book. First, that co-work is effective and efficient once its variables have been understood and incorporated into practice. It is time-consuming, arduous and may not be the most economical means of groupwork but it can be rewarding for clients and leaders. Secondly, that single leadership may appear daunting but is a viable and effective method of working with groups providing that practitioners possess a framework for practice and are aware of their reasons for choosing this modality. It is not to be undertaken lightly but may not hold the terrors which practitioners often seek to avoid by choosing co-leadership as their preferred method. Whichever method is adopted, the skills and processes involved in groupwork are not dissimilar to those involved in other methods of intervention. This book seeks to explore the pragmatic and therapeutic potential of each in the belief that practitioners should be well-grounded in the techniques, advantages and limitations of each approach.

This book has been shaped by my groupwork practice and teaching and by an extensive survey of group leaders within Family Service Units (Preston-Shoot, 1986). An author cannot guarantee success. However, some conditions and procedures facilitate effective groupwork, some undermine it. By exploring all the stages involved in working with groups, perhaps a contribution can be made towards improved understanding of and practice in this method of work which should form one of a range of interventions available to practitioners.

2

Types and Purposes of Groups

Introduction

In this chapter groups and what they may be used for will be introduced. By discussing the various types of groups, their purposes and applications, practitioners may be encouraged to be clear about what type of group they envisage – the first stage in effective groupwork. This requires that they identify their main and secondary purposes for a group and the values and theoretical frameworks which they are seeking to apply.

What is a group?

Groups vary greatly in character and type. They can be long- or short-term, on-going or time-limited, with a closed or open membership. They may be led by one person or more and rely on open or topic-orientated discussion or on exercises and games. They may aim to foster support or social interaction, or to provide opportunities for members to develop their potential abilities, to use untapped personal resources or to resolve particular problems. They may focus on common problems experienced by members outside the group or on issues and difficulties experienced by members within the group. Alternatively, they may be orientated towards social action, focussing their efforts on problems or circumstances which may or may not be experienced by members but which have implications beyond the group itself. Groups can be formed, with members drawn together by social workers, where membership may be compulsory or arise from an offer and acceptance of this offer. Other groups arise spontaneously, members coming together through circumstances or common concerns such as housing or community facilities, rather than through the interventions of an outsider. Some groups are small, allow face-to-face contact and encourage the formation of relationships which foster mutual identification and influence. Other groups are large and less intimate, where mutual identification occurs not through meeting but through some interest, common bond or characteristic. Groups also are a naturally occurring phenomena within the life cycle of every individual. These groups include the family, school classes, peer-groups, political parties and professional or staff groups. This variety in size, origins and purposes makes definition complex.

This book will examine one variety of group with which social workers are concerned. This is a group whose members choose to involve or agree to the intervention of a social worker and where the leaders have a professional duty and obligation to these members. It is a group where the leaders may or may not have been responsible for its formation but where their role is to help members work together and achieve the group's aims.

How may this group be defined further? First, it is a collection of people who spend some time together, who see themselves as members of a group and who are identified as members by outsiders. By definition, therefore, this includes groups formed by social workers and pre-existing groups where members have come together and where the social worker chooses to intervene. Two examples of pre-existing groups are a tenants' group formed by residents for the purpose of campaigning for improved housing conditions and a group of individuals with mental handicaps formed from a hospital population for the purpose of preparing them for living in group homes. The definition requires members to have some physical proximity and implies recognition of the boundaries of the group.

Secondly, members may or may not expect to continue meeting indefinitely. Some groups are time-limited, the duration fixed by the groupworkers. The length of others may be determined by progress within the group towards a stated aim, for example preparation for group home living. In on-going groups circumstances such as age, interest, need or physical location will shape attendance, with members rather than groupworkers taking responsibility for the length of their membership of the group.

Thirdly, direct interactions and exchanges are possible between members who are interdependent. This requires physical proximity and restricts the size of the group. It implies that a group is not an alternative setting for one-to-one social work but a context where each member experiences several interpersonal relationships which, together with the members' contributions and the group's dynamics, may be used to help members reach their goals as individuals and for the group. Put another way, the work is not only with individual members as individuals but also with the way they organise their interactions and interdependency (Davies, 1975). This part of the definition implies too that the group's progress depends on the contribution of the total membership, on their capacity to act as a group towards the stated aims. Accordingly, not only do members need to work co-operatively but also they should understand and accept the purposes towards which they are working.

Fourthly, the group is established for one or more purposes. It has been said that members should share a common goal, this shared purpose providing a reason for members to invest and interact in the group and increasing a sense of unity (Heap, 1977). Certainly, shared goals and mutually agreed tasks positively correlate with the workers' performance. Mutual expectations and agreement on the means of achieving the group's goals positively influence group functioning and members' satisfaction and motivation (Maluccio and Marlow, 1974). Indeed, group members may share common interests from which they develop a sense of identity or unity which defines the group to others and legitimises its existence.

However, especially at the beginning of a group, members may not share a common goal. For example, in an Intermediate Treatment group, perhaps where membership is compulsory, members may hold different attitudes to and goals for the group which, in turn, may differ from the workers' purposes. I question whether it is necessary, say in social groups, to have a common purpose for members to feel valued for their contribution, to value other members or to experience a sense of belonging to the group. Indeed, mutual agreement about goals is neither necessary for nor a guarantee of purposive activity and successful outcomes. It may be contra-indicated in terms of the time and energy spent to achieve it (Macarov, 1974). Agreement may be difficult to establish, especially in the beginning, but this does not preclude working together. If groups are formed where members and leaders disagree on their objectives in coming together, where the leaders find themselves opposed to the group's objectives, or where members' purposes differ, two conditions are required for effective groupwork. Some agreement is necessary about short- or medium-term objectives if the group is to be established, a reasonable consensus among members concerning what the group is for and how to proceed, on the rights and duties of members and leaders, and on guidelines for behaviour in the group. Aims should be realistic and feasible, with differences respected and contained in the group. Further, it should feel possible to work with the differences and towards a greater consensus in the group. Otherwise, it may prove difficult for the group to achieve its potential (Whitaker, 1975). Thus, a contract or purposes of the group may fall into one of four categories (Preston-Shoot *et al.*, 1984):

- preliminary contract: an agreement to survey what is being offered without commitment and to clarify expectations.
- primary contract: a mutual agreement based on a common definition of the goals.
- interim agreement: a trial period either because aims are

not agreed or to establish whether the services offered are appropriate to the needs defined.
- reciprocal agreements: in which workers and members accept that their purposes are not identical but agree to co-operate in helping each other achieve their different goals.

Fifthly, groups with which social workers interact may or may not be congruent with the function or views of their employing agency. Since the support of colleagues is a necessary condition for effective groupwork, practitioners may adopt an approach which they believe their colleagues and agency will accept, one which is compatible with agency function, resources and expectations (Brown *et al.*, 1982). Alternatively, they can devise a project which they consider to be ethical and effective and then attempt to persuade their colleagues and organisation to endorse the proposal. This may involve them in campaigning to change the attitudes and traditional approaches of their own organisation (Mullender and Ward, 1985). Social workers may find that they are encouraged to develop innovative approaches with client groups who appear not to respond to one-to-one casework or who add significantly to their agency's workloads. Equally, they may encounter indifference, mistrust or hostility shown in the absence of referrals or the referral of unsuitable clients. It is prudent to explore ideas with colleagues with the aim of arriving at a consensus about the place of groupwork and the members who might benefit. Through discussing with colleagues their views, reservations and concerns, groupworkers will be able to assess whether their project will be effective in their work environment and whether it will involve isolation from or rejection by colleagues.

Besides the support of colleagues, a group is more likely to succeed if the workers are interested in the group and if it originates in demand or unmet need rather than in a worker's wish to develop or find expression. Of course, there may be occasions when a groupwork project is devised for staff or student training or to try a new approach in response to old, familiar problems. However, a group is more likely to take off when it is based on an assessment of being an effective way to meet a situation. Therefore, a preliminary to an effective group is research into client and worker opinions from which a statement can be made of the needs identified by clients and professionals, the resources already available and the gaps in service provision. Put another way, a group should be a response to clients rather than clients being created for a group to serve an initiative.

It will be apparent that these part-definitions apply to a wide variety of groups. Similarly, definitions of groupwork which refer to enhancing social functioning or helping members to cope more effectively with personal, social or environmental difficulties can embrace a wide variety of types of groups and more specific objectives. Consequently, to make sense of the term groupwork and to facilitate clear thinking and practice, social workers need to classify types of groups. From this classification they can determine the type of group they envisage or are interested in.

The categories which follow are not mutually exclusive since one type can contain elements of another type. What will emerge too is the interplay between the main activity of the group, the style of the groupworkers and the purpose of the group. The purpose of the group dictates the nature of the group and, to some extent at least, the style of the leaders. The nature of the group is dictated by the way the members or leaders perceive the purpose of the group.

Types of groups

Social groups

These groups are defined by their content: social or recreational activities. The purpose of these groups may be to overcome members' isolation, to provide a positive experience of relationships, or more simply to offer an opportunity for pleasure. The groupworkers may assume responsibility for the group's activities or seek to encourage members both to offer suggestions and to contribute their own resources and skills for the benefit of other members. Members may be encouraged to take responsibility for parts of the group in the belief that this, together with enabling members to develop their interests and skills, can increase their sense of fulfilment and self-worth. Examples are social clubs for ex-psychiatric patients and old people, day centres and youth clubs.

Group psychotherapy

These groups aim to effect symptom relief and basic personality change. The emphasis is on enabling members to achieve their individual therapeutic goals. A variety of problems can be tackled effectively in group psychotherapy. Common among these are self-concepts like low self-esteem, lack of purpose and direction, and lack of a clear identity. Members may bring symptoms of anxiety, depression, ineffective coping with stress or poor performance at work. They may complain of emotional difficulties like the inability to express feelings or poor control over emotions. They may locate their difficulties in interpersonal functioning, usually described as the inability to achieve intimacy, discomfort in group situations or lack of trust.

Members need to be motivated, wanting to change and prepared to work for it through self-exploration. Their wish to join the group should be voluntary and not the result of external pressure. They need to believe that the group will suit them and to accept the rationale on which group psychotherapy is founded. Since these groups rely heavily on verbal communication, members should be able to use verbal skills. A final requirement is psychological-mindedness, an ability to accept an appropriate psychological explanation of interactions and relationships within the self and between the self and others.

These groups have a present orientation, a here and now focus on what actually happens in the group between members, between them and the leaders and between them and the group. There is a future orientation too, a focus on the goals of individual members, the options they possess, how they might choose from these and translate the choice into action. A focus on events which occur outside the group is discouraged as is excessive historical enquiry into the origins of members' behaviour. The rationale for this process is that members can be helped to see that they are not unique, that they can derive support from the other members as a result of which their resistance will decrease and they can be encouraged to take risks. A further rationale is that members' behaviour in the group will be a direct reflection of their behaviour in life generally. These groups aim to enable members to become aware of their characteristic behaviours, with change coming about from a recognition of the ways members relate in the group and from using the encouragement and reinforcement of the group to try out new ways of relating both within and outside the group. In this process the leaders attempt to steer the group into a here and now focus and may direct their comments either to individuals, sub-groups or the whole group.

A fuller explanation of group psychotherapy may be found in the writings of Bion (1961), Yalom (1970), Foulkes and Anthony (1973) and Bloch (1979).

Group counselling

These groups focus on resolving particular problems or modifying specific situations. Usually members share a common problem which provides the focus of the group. Focus is maintained on this problem, which is identified clearly, and little attention is paid to other problems unless the group agrees to expand the focus. The problems may be practical and material, for example negotiating one's way through organisations dealing with welfare benefits, or they may be emotional and interpersonal. Here examples would include groups focussing on depression, isolation, children who are beyond the control of their parents or difficulties facing step-parents on joining a family. One task for the workers is to help members identify and keep to the focus of the group. Another is to enable members to build links between themselves. The groupworkers seek to enable the group to clarify the problem, to share solutions adopted by individual members and to help members individually and as a group to take decisions and to develop behaviours which relate to the demands of the situation. In focussing on the problem and the feelings which members hold in relation to it, environmental factors should not be overlooked either as contributory factors to the problem or as targets for change.

Educational groups

In one form of educational group, the purpose is to offer information and to impart skills through direct instruction. For example, a benefits group might aim to inform members of their welfare rights and to instruct them on how they may obtain these rights. A practical skills group might aim to introduce members to easier ways of dealing with practical problems in the home when on a low income and to provide an environment where basic skills are acquired through practice.

In another form, the purpose is to orientate and prepare members for life stages, new experiences and challenges, the prospect of which may arouse fear, uncertainty or disorientation. These groups focus on a change in status or position and work through the feelings aroused by transitions: from junior to secondary school, from school into employment, from early adulthood into mid-life, from work into retirement or unemployment. Groups consisting of psychiatric patients awaiting discharge into the community, prospective foster parents or couples awaiting the arrival of their first child may fall into this category. There may be some information-giving but the emphasis is usually on developing abilities and behaviours which have been underused or not needed previously.

In leading such groups, it is important to consider how people learn. Effective learning is less likely to come from without, from knowledge being transmitted in a teacher – pupil format. It is more likely to follow from members' willingness to engage in shared learning to resolve difficulties felt by them to be real. It is more likely to follow from a willingness to participate in a process of discovery and enquiry in which members contribute their own experiences, offer their ideas to a shared learning process, acquire support from the group and through discussion or simulation exercises consider how to approach the situation which they are facing.

Social treatment groups

This cluster of groups, of which Intermediate Treatment may be the most familiar, may be sub-divided into four:

First, groups aiming to maintain adaptive patterns of behaviour and functioning or to enhance social functioning which is apparent already. These groups have a reinforcement and supportive orientation.

Secondly, groups aiming to modify patterns of behaviour and functioning which may be disabling the individual. These groups have a change orientation. The purpose may be to enable individual members to give up redundant behaviours, adaptations which they have continued to repeat after they have lost their meaning or to apply out of the context in which they were serviceable. Alternatively, the purpose may be to encourage members to give up behaviours which are defined as deviant and unacceptable.

Thirdly, problem-centred groups aiming to improve members' abilities to handle and resolve their problems. The group is concerned with specific difficulties located either within or external to the individual members. The group process and the influence of group members are used to achieve this aim. Examples include social skills groups, Intermediate Treatment and groups for sexually abused children.

Fourthly, compensatory groups. Here the aim is not so much to effect change but, through using activities, to provide members with life experiences which they have missed or to compensate for deprivation. Activity groups for children are one example of this type of group.

Discussion groups

In these groups the focus is on the general rather than the particular, on topics of interest to members rather than on specific difficulties or problems. The groupworkers' task is to create an atmosphere of trust and support in the group so that members may voice and develop their interests and use the contributions of other members.

Self-help groups

These groups have a variety of aims, from campaigning for attitude or social change to using the group's resources for support and individual problem-resolution. However, whatever the group's purposes, the groupworkers aim to become less central in or less responsible for the work of the group, often to the point of the group meeting without them. Thus, a women's self-help group might have the following aims:
- to provide an opportunity for women to have fun and enjoy each other;
- to help women feel more confident and more in control of their own lives;
- to facilitate ways in which women can recognise and care better for their own needs;
- to help women communicate their feelings and needs to others and learn to give and receive support;
- to use group processes to understand what kinds of blocks and barriers exist which prevent women getting the support, care and nurture which they need;
- to establish a forum in which women can continue to meet.

Social action groups

Many people, whether or not they are clients of social welfare agencies, are trapped in social and economic deprivation. Social action groups aim to utilise a group's resources for collective power as a vehicle for campaigning for social change and for the rights as well as the needs of group members. These groups often form around issues like housing standards, community facilities or welfare rights.

Self-directed groups

In the groups described above, the aims are identified either by the groupworkers or by them in conjunction with the group's members. In self-directed groups, described by Mullender and Ward (1985), members rather than groupworkers determine the direction and objectives of the group. These groups may be problem-centred, focussing on problems which members raise. They require, as do self-help groups, that members work together and find their own solutions, not just from within the resources of the group members but through attempting to change people outside the group. Like social action groups, they may campaign on issues arising from members' concerns expressed once the group has formed. A key goal often is some aspect of external change together with the development of members' self-esteem and assertiveness. The group identifies the skills, knowledge and abilities within it and these are harnessed to enable members to work on the issues which the group has identified.

From this classification it will have become clear that groupwork can address a variety of aims and purposes and that the types are not mutually exclusive. Rather, a particular design can incorporate features of several types of groups. Therefore, the first task for practitioners who intend to lead a group is to identify the type of group they wish to conduct. What type of group is it?

In selecting from this classification, groupworkers will be influenced by the goals they have in mind, the style of work and leadership which they favour and the assumptions and value-base which underpin their social work practice. The remainder of this chapter is devoted to these areas. Determining the type of group will be shaped by the objectives and aims with which the groupworkers begin and which will be influenced and modified through a dialogue with members when the social workers offer their services to an existing group or interview prospective members referred to a group which they are hoping to form. Having achieved a degree of clarity on the type of group to be conducted and the aims for that group, questions of structure such as size, duration and open or closed membership can be resolved.

Aims, purposes and uses of groupwork

Groupwork does have its limitations. Generally, groups cannot provide exclusive attention to an individual member. Nor are they an alternative setting for one-to-one work with the addition of an audience. Whether a group has goals which are defined in terms of social action, individual-centred or group-centred aims, members will be required to work co-operatively towards these ends and, consequently, to put aside on occasions their needs or issues for the work of the group or for other members.

Nor can groups be expected to provide immediate benefits. Placing a number of people together does not mean that they function immediately as a group rather than a collection of individuals. If, for example, one aim is that members will discover that they share experiences in common, the discovery of such commonality may take several meetings to emerge. If one aim is to encourage members to verbalise their feelings associated with their difficulties or circumstances, an atmosphere of trust has to be fostered before they are likely to feel that it is safe to do so. Whether or not members ultimately feel that the group is beneficial depends on their commitment and the groupworkers' skills in promoting the functioning of the group.

The economic motive is questionable too. Social workers may believe that their service-delivery will be improved by seeing several people at once. However, this apparently economical approach involves considerable time and emotional commitment which should not be incorporated into overstretched workloads. Moreover, groups do not achieve necessarily the aims which influence social workers to form them nor reduce the demands that members may make on social work agencies. Indeed, the reverse may be the case. Accordingly, groupwork should be adopted when social workers consider it to be the best method available for tackling a problem or achieving a particular goal rather than as a numbers' exercise alone.

Another motive which social workers may have for using groupwork is to reduce the powerlessness, isolation and stigma attached to members as individuals and as clients. Certainly, members may gain considerably from meeting with other members. It is not uncommon to hear clients express relief at the realisation that they are not alone in their particular situation, that they are acceptable and have skills, knowledge and abilities which are valued, useful and acceptable. They may feel less threatened by social workers, having other members for support. Further, a group may find it easier than individuals alone to challenge and alter the labels, perceptions and attitudes held by those outside the group. However, bringing together clients in a group may increase their sense of separation and difference from individuals and groups which do not share their circumstances and problems (Davies, 1975). It may reinforce the labels attached to them and widen rather than narrow social gaps. Thus, social workers need to consider carefully how members of a group might feel or perform within and outside the group and whether the benefits which might accrue from membership outweigh the perceptions which members and others might attach to them by virtue of their membership. Belonging to a group, of itself, does not change descriptions applied to members by themselves or by others.

So what are the uses to which groupwork can be put? What aims and purposes can groups work towards and achieve? It is likely that a group will have several aims drawn from across the categories described below.

One set of purposes may be described as preventive. The problem of isolation may be tackled by the formation of a group with the aim of reducing its effects. Members may feel less alone by meeting others with similar interests or circumstances. Achieving a sense of belonging and mutual identity can lead to change in social relationships and to members being able to receive help or tackle situations or problems using the support, knowledge, ideas and experience acquired in the group. This preventive function may be seen too in groups which aim to maintain or improve functioning, for example in social skills, parent and toddler and Intermediate Treatment groups where a programme is designed to enable members to develop more adaptive and functional patterns of behaviour or interaction.

Another use for groupwork may be defined as the purpose of achieving external change, of encouraging social action in the community in the pursuit of social change goals.

No social worker can be unaware that the systems of which individual clients are a part and in which they live and function exert a considerable, often negative influence. Nor can social workers be unfamiliar with the feelings of powerlessness and alienation which clients experience, particularly in a decade which has seen the emergence of the issue of clients' rights through campaigns for open records and client participation at case conferences. Unemployment, poor housing, poverty, and inadequate community resources all impinge on the clients of social work agencies. If social workers neglect these features, they omit an important, influential part of the reality of their clients' lives and limit the extent and impact of their change efforts.

Groups which incorporate the purpose of social action aim to challenge received assumptions concerning the powerful and powerless. They redefine clients' needs as clients' rights and hope to achieve improvements in their environment and living conditions. Social action groups campaign on issues, establish provisions such as social clubs and playgroups, and interact with representatives of such agencies as the police and housing departments. Members often select the targets of change themselves. If the attitudes or behaviour of the members change, this is seen as occurring through the emphasis on and achievement of social action as opposed to concentration on these attitudes and behaviours themselves. A specific aim within the overall purpose of social change goals is to improve communication and interaction between members and between them and the systems outside the group. A further subsidiary aim is to achieve a change in the way other systems perceive group members. If this is achieved, a change may follow in how members perceive themselves.

The leaders of groups with social change goals have several tasks. One is to ensure that such goals are realistic and to contribute their knowledge and experience to help the group in setting and pursuing its goals. A second is to place responsibility on group members for decisions, action and support from which confidence in their own abilities and efforts may increase.

Another set of aims may be defined as group-centred. The objectives of the group are derived from problems experienced by the group prior to or outside the workers' involvement with it. The group is used as a therapeutic resource, that is the resources of group members and group-workers are used to achieve the group's objectives. A group may act together for effectiveness, using its collective intellectual and emotional resources to achieve social change goals or to demonstrate how others can act helpfully towards members. Equally, the objective might be to establish a self-help forum where the goals might include enriching the lives of the members or improving relationships with peers.

Another cluster of aims may be defined as individual-centred and described in a number of ways. They may take the form of helping members understand and develop the resources to live with, lessen or eradicate personal problems of social functioning which cause them to experience their lives as unsatisfactory, difficult to manage, lacking in quality or unacceptable to others (Brown *et al.*, 1982). Thus, the aim may be expressed as the achievement of insight, defined as the exploration of feelings, the acquisition of understanding into their own and others' motivation behind behaviour and into self-defeating ways of dealing with problems. Alternatively, the aim may be defined in terms of individual development, often referred to as treatment. Here the effort may be directed towards developing new ways of behaving to overcome obstacles to social development and growth, with the group providing opportunities to rehearse these. The emphasis may be on narrowing the gap between potential and actual functioning, for example in a group aiming to prepare toddlers for school. Or again, the aim may be specified as providing missing life experiences or enabling members to adopt new roles to improve their social functioning. The emphasis is on individual change, the focus being problems which members share but experience individually outside the group. Whether described as aiming for increased self-esteem, improved capacity to relate to others or increased ability to use personal skills and resources, the objective is personality change, either behavioural, emotional or attitudinal.

A second task for practitioners intending to run a group is to formulate a general aim or purpose. Having identified the needs, problems or circumstances which might become a focus or target, what is the group's main purpose? Are there any secondary purposes? These broad aims are a starting point for interacting with potential members. They may be modified and sharpened into specific objectives for the group as a whole and for individual members in the light of referrals, discussions with members and the resources actually available in the group. The rationale for defining initial purposes is that if the leaders are unclear, they may give confused messages to the group on the degree of participation required and on acceptable or potential goals. Furthermore, the more the groupworkers are able to establish clear, initial purposes, the better they will be able to give members a clear basis for discussing their view of the group's purpose and accepting the offer of a group and the intervention of social workers. They will be better placed to make alternative or supplementary suggestions regarding aims and to consider whether the group will satisfy their perception of their needs and situation.

Theoretical frameworks, styles of work and leadership

In this process of formulating the type of, and purpose for, a group, and later in understanding the group's dynamics and guiding their interaction with the group, practitioners will be influenced by the theoretical frameworks and styles of work and leadership felt by them to be congenial.

Social workers may use a psychological theoretical base. This may take the form of a psychodynamic understanding and interpretation of the group, for example using the framework that the group's work task is hindered but sometimes furthered by emotional drives, unconscious basic assumptions of fight-flight, pairing and dependency (Bion, 1961; McCullough and Ely, 1968). Equally, this psychodynamic understanding can be applied to individual members' experiences of and behaviour in groups, for instance in exploring the defence mechanisms used by them in a group. Alternatively, this theoretical base may be expressed through behaviour modification techniques such as homework, role rehearsal and positive reinforcement programmes or through an emphasis on feelings and self-disclosure as exemplified in the encounter movement and other 'new' therapies. Here games, role-plays, exercises, art and drama are used to promote social and personal development and the flow of effective communication.

Social workers may use a sociological theoretical base to inform their practice, emphasising a structural analysis of members' difficulties or circumstances rather than locating difficulties within the members themselves. They may emphasise power issues and the labelling process, with a group providing the opportunity for changing roles and interactions between members and between them and outsiders.

Social workers may use a systems approach, that is viewing the group as a system, each member as a sub-system within it and the group part of a wider network or super-system. Here the groupworkers may focus on the input and output of the system or on the effect on the group and individual members of the outside environment and on the relationships between individuals and sub-groups within the group. With a systemic perspective groupworkers view each system as having a purpose or goal. This is discovered through formulating and testing hypotheses which are neither true nor false but more or less useful and used as a basis for intervention without reference to their truth. Data is collected which will either validate, disconfirm or modify each hypothesis. Hypothesising enables the groupworkers to track interactional patterns both within the group and between it and systems outside the group, to involve every member and to establish how the group's organisation and behaviour fit together. The rationale is that individual change can occur only after a change in the system.

No one theoretical model is superior to the others and, indeed, an eclectic frame of reference provides greater flexibility in response to the multiple causation of members' difficulties and the many influences on the group's processes.

The purpose in identifying theoretical frameworks is three-fold. A lack of clarity can create confusion for leaders and members about what the group can and cannot achieve. Second, theoretical frameworks will shape the methods practitioners use in a group and may lead them away from enabling the group to pursue other aims. For instance, a psycho-dynamically-oriented groupworker is unlikely to emphasise social change goals which, however, may feel relevant to the members. Finally, frameworks can make sense of the group's dynamics.

Therefore, practitioners have a third task: to familiarise themselves with the theoretical models available and how these concepts shape how they operate and influence their styles of work and leadership. Thus (Hodge, 1985):

- what frames of reference do I use in my approach to groupwork?
- what do I understand by the term group dynamics? What understanding do I have about the dynamics of behaviour in and between groups?
- what theoretical studies have influenced my thinking about groupwork?
- what is my preferred way of working in groups (promoting discussion, organising activities, commenting on dynamics)?
- what do I see as the tasks and responsibilities of group-workers?
- what style is most congenial to me? Will this enable me to achieve the broad aims of the group?
- what is the appropriate leadership style of this group (introducing topics, interpreting the group process, using self-disclosure)?
- do I see myself as determining the group's aims or is this to be shared with members or are they to be given this task? (Hodge, 1985)

Groupworkers' values

So far this chapter has concentrated on 'facts': the types of groups available, their possible purposes and the theoretical frameworks which shape practice. However, this emphasis should not neglect values. Social work is always value-laden since it is bound into political, economic and theoretical settings. These values influence how practitioners formulate, plan and lead groups. For example, if one aim of a group is adjustment, this implies acceptance of conventional values rather than attempts to change this view of reality. If social workers ignore or are confused about their values, the goals they formulate may not be relevant to what members bring to groups. They may be unable to take up what members say affects them and their received ideas and assumptions will remain unchallenged.

Groupwork is a process of enquiry and discovery in which all participants are prepared to engage. It is a shared endeavour towards resolving problems or circumstances felt by participants to be both real and urgent. This view is based on a number of assumptions.

First, group members have the ability to be self-directing and have a responsibility for the direction of their learning and change-efforts. This encompasses a belief that members should have some say over their lives and that they have a capacity to diagnose their own needs and decide from a range of possibilities. Clients have rights and should be involved in all stages of the social work process: taking part in decision making; having the opportunity to present their views and the right to know the grounds on which decisions are taken (BASW, 1980; Barclay, 1982; FSU, 1982). Applying these principles to groupwork, the groupworkers' task is to ensure that clients are aware of their rights and how to obtain them, of what groups can achieve and the range of alternatives, and are enabled to define their wants and needs in the group. That is, they should participate in formulating the group's aims and groupworkers should be interested in their views since they are involved in a process of learning, change and development to which members can contribute. The extent of this participation may vary. However, even with young children, people with mental handicaps and offenders for whom groupwork is one aspect of a statutory involvement, groupworkers should not underestimate members' abilities or under-value their rights and should seek to enable them to voice concerns and take action on them. For example, in groupwork with offenders, it is appropriate not only to focus on changing members' attitudes towards offending but also on enabling them to take up their concerns which they see as contributing to their situation such as policing activities.

The second assumption is that members' experiences are significant and that a group should begin with and respect these. Members will have critical powers, skills, knowledge and abilities to offer each other, resources on which the group can draw for support, learning and collective action. If members' experiences are devalued or ignored, this creates an atmosphere in which the assumption flourishes that they are passive recipients. It denies a part of their identity. A group should encourage and enable members to identify the capacities they are bringing to it with which they can help each other. This value principle assumes that members' statements are not necessarily symptoms of illness or deviance but those of ordinary people facing particular circumstances.

There are difficulties in implementing practice on the basis of this assumption. It is not always possible to know when client opinion has been understood. Members may be over-eager to agree with the groupworkers or may voice what they believe is expected of them in order to fulfil roles they anticipate are expected of them or to avoid embarrassment. The characteristics of the groupworkers, help received in past encounters and their knowledge of services and groups may shape how they present their experiences and relate to the group. They may have experienced feelings of powerlessness, isolation and hopelessness that arise by virtue of being clients and the more disadvantaged members of society. Therefore, they may need encouragement and a clearly articulated belief from groupworkers, which they demonstrate in their practice, that participation can alter these features significantly, that members can address the power and control which others have over their lives by questioning others' attitudes to them, by challenging norms and by being involved in decision-making.

The third assumption is that groupworkers are not experts

who alone possess an understanding of the needs and dynamics of a group and its members but are facilitators and resources in a process of enquiry and development. They may put forward their knowledge, opinions and experience and they may be responsible for the group's programme. However, this assumption requires a redefinition of the workers' expertise so that it becomes seen as a capacity to engage the group in exchanging and developing knowledge and skills to meet its tasks, to help members understand their problems and identify methods of tackling these collectively or personally. Group members may be unwilling to relinquish a view of the groupworkers as experts and leaders or unable to accept that the leaders do not have solutions to prevent, manage or eradicate problems.

Closely connected with this value stance is the concept of authority. The fourth assumption is that groupworkers should examine this concept from the members' perspective. The concept may be defined in four ways:

1. positional: authority conveyed by the position groupworkers hold, for example in statutory orders.
2. a representative of others: delegated organisational authority where the organisation has ultimate power and authority.
3. sapiential: authority from experience, professional knowledge and skills.
4. influence or example: authority given by members to the groupworkers because they see them as an appropriate model.

Groupworkers can hold authority in any or all of these categories at the same time. However, how they view their authority may differ from how agencies or members see it. The value position laid out emphasises the third and fourth definitions, which groupworkers commonly see as enabling them to practise groupwork effectively. However, members may see the groupworkers' authority as of the first two types and groupworkers may find themselves having to exercise these types of authority. Some focus may be necessary on differences in perceptions of the groupworkers' authority and pertinent questions here include:

- where would I reflect the standards and authority of the agency?
- where do I consider it appropriate to mirror society and where to question it?
- to whom do I feel that I owe allegiance in the final analysis: to clients or to my employer?
- which values imposed by organisations would I agree with even where they are not accepted by clients? Which would I dispute?

The final assumption is that groupworkers should value self-knowledge and address structural, interpersonal and intrapersonal perspectives. Groupwork should not become a blanket focus on personal pathology or social action; rather it should address both each individual and the systems within which they function. In other words, individual difficulties or circumstances have a public, political context; economic circumstances have individual repercussions and interpersonal dynamics have private and structural components. Groupworkers need to consider each.

In considering the application of their values to their groupwork practice, several questions suggest themselves:

- what am I trying to do? What am I capable of?
- is my approach microist, a symptom approach focussing on the individual's experience; or is it macroist, tackling causes and policy issues; or is it a mixture of the two? Where do I propose to intervene?
- ought I to be involved in this process? Am I supporting the status quo and conventional norms or aiming for social change?

Conclusion

This chapter has presented a definition of a group and a classification of types and purposes of groups. Four tasks that intending groupworkers should undertake have been identified, namely to answer:

- what type of group is it?
- what are the aims of the group?

– what theoretical frameworks are available and influencing practice?
– what values are practitioners applying?

In the next chapter this initial thinking will be taken further by working through the stages in planning a group.

3

Planning the Group

Introduction

Having decided on the type of group and broad aims, the next step is to devote time to planning and the formation of the group. The future effectiveness of any group depends on thorough preparation and planning, which are complex tasks. To illustrate this complexity, how should groupworkers respond to contacts from group members between sessions? How should they divide their tasks or negotiate their authority with the group in a way which will not confuse the members or result in conflicts and tensions being played out in the group? How should members be selected and what should groupworkers do if too many or too few referrals are received? What is the inter-relationship between the group's task and size? If this inter-relationship is misconstrued, some members may be left uninvolved or underinvolved in the group's tasks which may prevent the group attaining its goals. Through planning the group practitioners can reflect on and decide their approach to questions concerning the group's structure and operation. If insufficient time or thought is given to planning, leaders may find that their plans are too ambitious or too confusing and threatening for the members. Alternatively, they may experience their leadership as muddled and uncertain, with a consequent loss of confidence in their skills and abilities.

This chapter will focus on the three major components in planning, namely membership of the group, its operation, and factors external to it.

Membership of the group

When considering questions relating to a group's membership, it is helpful it groupworkers are clear on the type of group they wish to conduct or are interacting with, and on the structure most useful to potential members. If unsure about this, preparatory discussions with members can be used to explore the possibilities and any preferences which the participants might have.

Open or closed membership?

This depends very much on the purpose and type of group. Social groups may not be disrupted by frequent changes in membership but task or goal-oriented groups may require a period of stability in order to develop and operate as a group and not to lose focus and continuity by having to deal with the feelings and fantasies surrounding the loss of members or the introduction of newcomers. A closed group does seem to promote cohesion and trust and may provide security for members who initially are apprehensive or lacking in confidence. However, a small group may cease to be viable if closed and if more than a few members leave or fail to attend regularly.

Where members are chosen on a homogeneous basis, that is where they have problems, needs or experiences in common, a closed group enables it to gel quickly. However, the learning opportunities in an open-ended or heterogeneous group should not be undervalued.

Where groupworkers are working with a pre-existing group or a given population, such as a tenants' group or groups in residential settings, it may not be possible to maintain the same membership over time. One possible response to this is to organise a closed group for a fixed period, adding new members at this point if some individuals have left. This allows the group a reasonable period to develop and operate as a group (Whitaker, 1975). If the group is closed but attendance is likely to be erratic, groupworkers can minimise the extent to which this might undermine the group's effectiveness by programming each session as an event in itself.

Number of members?

This depends on the purpose and type of group. For example, where the aim is to enable members to verbalise their feelings, a small group may be less threatening or, alternatively, may lead members to feel pressurised into describing their feelings and to become defensive. On the other hand, a large group can be a setting where reticent members can hide or where some members are uninvolved or underinvolved in the group's task. Consequently, any decision concerning the group's size should consider the resources and personalities of the potential members.

However, some general guidelines are available. The smaller the group, the greater the likelihood that one-to-one interaction between members or with the groupworkers will develop rather than interaction as a group. Further, there is a greater likelihood that intimacy will exist. However, task orientation is less likely and there is an increased possibility of disintegration because of absence or withdrawal from the group. The larger the group, the greater the likelihood is of sub-group formation or of a small grouping being very active surrounded by silent onlookers. In very large groups freedom of expression is reduced. In small groups, for instance where the aim is to enable members to develop their skills and their identity, there may be insufficient experience or energy to be creative or to offer alternative methods of tackling personal difficulties.

The ideal size for groups with therapeutic purposes, and where the aim is individual or community change, would appear to be between six and eight (Heap, 1977). This number seems to facilitate task orientation, the expression of disagreement and social interaction. Groupworkers may choose to recruit several additional members to allow for subsequent drop-outs.

Therefore, in considering size, the task is to create the optimum conditions for the group to achieve its purposes.

Accordingly, groupworkers should define size in relation to their aims and objectives prior to requesting referrals. Two difficulties are common here. First, particularly in groups which have formed naturally, groupworkers may have to work with a group which they consider to be too small or large for the tasks it is attempting to accomplish. One response to this is to discuss with the group whether and how to encourage other people to join or how the group is to structure its work to enable each member to be involved. Secondly, where social workers are forming groups, the number of eligible members may be small. It is tempting, but I feel inadvisable, to run the group where the number of members is felt to be too small for the tasks envisaged.

Workers' clients as members of the group?

There are several advantages to having own clients in a group. Social workers will have a greater awareness of their clients' needs and an opportunity to use existing positive relationships to provide initial reassurance for them within the group. Social workers will see how family members function outside their family. This may provide a more effective integration of groupwork with other services being offered.

However, these may not turn out to be advantages. Practitioners and clients have to adapt to the change of format and roles and the presence of own clients in a group can create difficulties of confidentiality, exclusive relationships or factionalism, resentment and rivalry (Yalom, 1970). Taking confidentiality, how should groupworkers respond to information given in a group about people outside it or outside the group about people within it? This is one aspect of a potential difficulty in keeping the roles and tasks of the contexts separate. This may be seen in members confiding in the groupworker but not in the group, using the group as an individual session with an audience. Or, it may be highlighted through members discussing problems which do not relate to the group's task, perhaps raising issues which can be followed up only outside the group. Moreover, other family members with whom the social worker interacts may feel excluded or threatened by the client's membership of a group run by their social worker. These feelings may interfere either with the family work or the client's membership of the group. Both client and groupworker also face the issue of what information or progress in respect of the group is to be shared with these significant others.

Nor are all relationships between caseworkers and clients positive. Negative past relationships and experiences might be brought into the group, reducing its effectiveness and the potential of relationships formed within it. Members may find the group difficult because of disappointed expectations that it is not identical to other contexts in which they meet with their social worker. Own clients as group members might generate conflict between those who have social workers and those who do not, or may create a situation where members relate more to their social worker than to the group or co-leader.

Groupworkers can use a variety of responses in these instances. Within the group they can bring other members into the conversation or use the co-worker more actively with clients of the other leader. They might direct members' comments into the group and decline to be drawn into an individual relationship during the session. It may be appropriate, especially where it seems to be creating difficulties, to discuss with members their feelings about the presence of the groupworkers' clients in the group. Prior to beginning the group it is useful to discuss with potential members and significant others the implications of membership for both the member, their family and for the social worker, what is to be shared about the group and how this will be done. Finally, co-workers should share their knowledge of potential members to ensure that each is able to take a full part in the group and avoid a secondary role.

Random selection of members or compositional criteria?

How are members to be selected? Selection is an intricate exercise. Unlikely combinations may work well, carefully selected groups may not. An ideal composition is not found easily. The attributes viewed as essential for membership will depend on the group's objectives which, therefore, should be outlined before leaders consider selection. Unless the potential membership is the totality of persons in a setting or is a pre-existing, already formed group, groupworkers should decide what characteristics are essential and desirable in potential members (Hodge, 1985; Muir, 1978). In other words, for whom is the group intended? What type of clients are most appropriate for the type of group planned? What resources within members are groupworkers looking for?

Answers to these questions will depend on the group's aims and the specific cluster of needs, problems or issues which are to be the target for intervention. Thus, age, gender, marital status, socio-economic circumstances, severity of problems, geographical location and specific personality qualities may or may not form part of the selection criteria. For example, a group may find the aim of breaking down isolation or establishing a self-help group unobtainable if members live too far apart. Likewise, in a discussion group, the ability to verbalise and to talk openly about emotional and social concerns may be crucial. In a group with social action goals, it is probably important that potential members have the resources for collective action and similar experiences concerning the target for intervention. It is necessary too that they are not so preoccupied with their individual difficulties or situations that they have little motivation for a co-operative effort.

Leaders should avoid any composition which isolates one individual. For instance, it is unwise to form a group consisting of one offender and the remainder non-offenders, or one man and the remainder women. This is because the isolated person may be scapegoated and may feel both exposed and vulnerable. Additionally, the individual tends not to be seen as an individual but as a representative of their grouping and thus risks being stereotyped by the others (Whitaker, 1975).

It is useful to think in terms of descriptive and behavioural characteristics. Descriptive characteristics include age, gender, marital status, occupation and relationship to the social work agency. Behavioural characteristics include ways in which the individuals act or may be expected to behave in the group. A third category is situational characteristics: the problems, difficulties, circumstances and emotional or social concerns which members have as individuals. When considering selection, groupworkers may choose either heterogeneity or homogeneity, that is difference or commonality. If the purpose of the group is support, homogeneous characteristics may be more important since this may help the group to gel. If the group's objective is personality change, a homogeneous composition, especially of behavioural characteristics, might encourage resistance and defensiveness in a group or reduce the range of experiences and choices open to members. Here a heterogeneous composition in terms of personality characteristics may prove more beneficial. Where the aim is personality change, groupworkers do not want members who are so similar that one solution is reinforced in the group. Nor, however, do they want members who are so different that they find interaction difficult. This is not the same as saying that groupworkers should avoid selecting people with common problems. Many successful groups are run for people with similar problems since such commonality fosters acceptance and the realisation that they are not unique. However, what is important is that they do not share the same approaches in dealing with their problems. Only careful preselection interviews will suggest a potentially viable composition. The choice depends on the workers' goals for the group but, generally, a variety of personalities works best for social comparison and learning (Whitaker, 1975).

However, should social workers select members for a group? If handled insensitively, the process of selection can reproduce and strengthen labels already attached to clients and contributing to their problems (Davies, 1975). However, not all potential members are able to function in every type of group. In my view, a sensitive way of handling selection is to use referral forms and to offer the group to prospective members since this requires the participants to be clear about and to discuss their aims and perceptions. Referral forms fulfil several purposes. They assist everyone in being clear about their aims and expectations and help

groupworkers to be specific in their planning and presenta-
tion of the group and in selecting members. They also
provide a baseline, an initial measure for evaluating the
outcome of the group and a starting point for negotiating a
contract, specific aims and a programme for the group with
members.

None the less, groupworkers may wish to avoid being too
specific about clients who might benefit from the group. This
vagueness in selection criteria might be based on a lack of
faith in identifying suitable clients or on a fear that specificity
will discourage referrals which are notoriously difficult to
obtain anyway. However, to a large extent, the group's
ultimate effectiveness will be determined by care at this
stage.

In designing a referral form, groupworkers need to decide
what they want to know and what questions they want to
ask. For example, do groupworkers need to know about
home circumstances, school performance, the degree of
co-operation expected and the member's family relationships? In the spirit of client involvement, groupworkers
should provide a description of the group they are proposing
which should include its possible aims, length, timing of
sessions and suggested rules on confidentiality. Furthermore, groupworkers should request that referrers complete
the referral form with the potential member and, to this end,
the questions should be phrased in such a way that the client
is responding. In addition, a brief statement should be
provided concerning how the referral form will be used.

Useful questions might include:

- what do you want or hope to gain from the group?
- how do you see this group fitting in with other services you
  are receiving?
- what do you think are your main difficulties?
- what have you tried to do about them?
- what particularly concerns or worries you?
- what would you like to be different?
- what do you think are the good things in your life?
- what skills and abilities would you have to offer the
  group?

- what does your social worker see as your main difficulties?
- what does your social worker hope that you will gain from the group?
- what problems have you and your social worker been working on?
- how does your social worker feel that the group will help you both with the problems you have been working on?
- what are the attitudes of your family to the group?
- how keen are you to join the group?
- what might you find difficult in the group?

Offering the group to prospective members

It is useful if groupworkers meet potential members before the group begins. To begin with, the group's effectiveness depends on the members being able to function in the type of group the leaders envisage. Even when this has been established, members may be ambivalent about the group. They may be suspicious or confused about the group's purpose, the roles which the groupworkers will adopt, and the nature of the participation expected of them. The stress of joining or uncertainty about the group's goals may lead them to be defensive, especially since similarities between members will become apparent only once the group has met. In a group where membership is to be compulsory or where the choice to join is coloured by the approval of significant others, a strong possibility exists of non-compliance and aggression which may be seen in superficial co-operation, silence or acting out. Preparatory interviews enable the groupworkers and potential members to recognise and discuss feelings and problems occasioned by the offer of a group. Almost certainly, this will need to be repeated in the first group meetings if the group's work is not to be sabotaged by non-attendance, superficial co-operation or unco-operative silence. However, preparatory interviews do provide the opportunity for members to discuss their reservations about the group or problems in taking up membership. They enable the groupworkers to assess the extent to which members share with them a similar definition of problems or aims and to ensure that false expectations are not raised and that the limits of their own and the agency's commitment are clear.

Before offering the group, groupworkers have several tasks. They need to decide how to present the group's aims realistically and clearly to avoid raising false expectations and in a manner which anticipates members' likely concerns, fears or uncertainties about it. The leaders must be clear about what the group may achieve and what it might involve for members. Another task is to decide how to discuss the group's purpose in a manner which will enable members to match this with their perceptions of their needs and to assimilate the rationale for the group. Finally, groupworkers should present what they believe they can offer the group, using their personal profiles which are discussed in Chapter Five. Where possible, co-workers should offer the group to members jointly since this prepares members for a triadic rather than dyadic relationship.

Preparatory interviews are a two-way process of clarification. What is discussed will depend on the purpose of the group. For instance, in a group where personal difficulties might be shared, it is important to assess how willing prospective members are to share their thoughts and feelings with others. Information given in the referral form provides a useful beginning for exploring members' expectations of the group and whether the leaders and potential members are out of step or share sufficient common ground. It provides too an opportunity for developing what members would like the group to do for them and for clarifying their difficulties, concerns and strengths. It is from this information that groupworkers can assess the resources of group members which will suggest whether the group's aims are feasible and attainable. Thus, in the interviews, the groupworkers communicate their purpose for the group, the objectives and structure they are proposing and what may happen in the group. Prospective members have an opportunity to outline their objectives should they join and to explore their reservations before deciding whether or not to join. These feelings may take the form of expecting that membership will prove stigmatising, depressing or threatening to

established ways of coping or that it will prove ineffective in achieving change. It may be necessary to meet more
than once before both groupworkers and members have a
shared basis on which to make a decision.

Where social workers plan to join a pre-existing group, at
this stage they offer themselves to the group. This involves
communicating what they believe the group can aim for and
achieve, how this might be done and how they might be able
to assist. Again, therefore, it is useful to compile a personal
profile. Here, the preparatory interview is an opportunity
for members to talk about how they view the group and for
the workers to assess whether they feel they can intervene
effectively.

On the basis of this exploration and negotiation, the
leaders can assess whether their original formulation, their
overall aim and main target for intervention need to be
adapted, after which they can formulate specific goals and a
programme for the group. The guiding principle is to be
realistic and not over-ambitious.

Whatever is negotiated and planned as a result of offering
the group will need to be re-examined once the group has
begun since expectations of the group and the reality may
differ and since it is only in the first meetings that the extent
of a consensus about the group will emerge clearly. In other
words, the actual experience of the group may require
alterations to be made. The final contract with the group and
individual members will emerge only after several sessions
of the group. When a contract is concluded, it should include:

- why members were referred
- basic rules for the group
- details about the structure and purpose of the group
- statements of the objectives, expectations and responsibilities of members and leaders. Here the objectives are
  specific targets which together comprise the group's purpose, subdivided into indicators which are pointers to the
  extent to which the objectives have been achieved.
- dates for reviewing the group's progress.

Contracts should be flexible enough to respond to developments in the group, hence the importance of reviews. Preferably they should be written with each member having a copy. They should be made with each individual and with the group as a whole. They provide a baseline against which to measure developments and outcomes.

Group operation

Once groupworkers have decided on the group's membership or agreed to work with a pre-existing group, they can consider how the group will operate: how long sessions should last, how long the group should run for, how sessions should be recorded and possible methods and leadership styles. These questions are easier to answer when groupworkers have clear aims and a view of the resources which members will be bringing to the group.

Duration and frequency of the group

In fixing the group's length, leaders must balance their own needs with ensuring the most successful outcome for the group. I suspect that often greater weight is given to the constraints on groupworkers such as the length of student placements, other work commitments and the duration for which they feel that they can sustain commitment to a group, than to a structure related to group development or anticipated to be reasonable for an adequate completion of the group's task. Other influences might include agency practice-wisdom or tradition, previous experience or a fear that long groups might encourage dependency.

If duration is not given any thought or is based on preconceptions and organisational pressures or is fixed arbitrarily, there is an increased likelihood that the duration decided upon may prove inadequate for the completion of the task and it may be impossible to extend the group's length. I believe that workers should attempt some calculation of the length of time a group might require to establish trust, engage in its tasks and achieve its aims. An alternative is an open-ended group or one where length is considered frequently with ending related to progress within the group. I would argue that duration should be determined by the purposes of the group and the members' resources rather than imposed on the group irrespective of intentions for the group. For example, where members already know each other or have formed already into a group, the time needed for trust to develop and for members to engage will be shorter than if the group is formed of strangers who will need to build trust before the work of the group can begin. This is not to suggest that short-term groups are inadvisable. Indeed, they can be useful for specific tasks such as focussing on transitions in members' lives or where the groupworkers want to learn more about a particular issue or difficulty as it affects and is experienced by members prior to devising a longer-term groupwork provision. However, I am suggesting that the time fixed should allow for both progression and regression since a group's progress is rarely a straightforward progression. It should allow for members to engage and negotiate the stages of a group described in Chapter Six. Otherwise, the group may terminate at the point where it is beginning to address its tasks.

The same degree of thought needs to be given to the length of meetings. Many groups seem to meet for one-and-a-half or two hours. Again, I believe that the length of sessions should be determined by members' resources, for example concentration and the need to settle and engage, and the group's aims. The time allowed should be based on the time required to enable the work to be completed coupled with practical points such as the availability of rooms and the leaders' time constraints. There is also the question of whether sessions should be of a fixed length. This has the disadvantage of possibly cutting through interaction inopportunely. However, the advantages are security and boundaries for members and the ability to plan time after the group. This decision should be based on what is likely to promote the group's work.

Two other questions arise here. First, how is the time

available to be structured? Is the session to be sub-divided, a technique especially useful in children's groups where their concentration on one task is limited? Again, the structure should be determined by the resources which members bring to the group and the objectives being pursued. Secondly, what is to be the frequency of meetings? This too depends on members' resources and the group's tasks. Some support groups may not need to meet weekly and less frequent meetings may be indicated where members are to be encouraged to complete tasks between sessions. In other groups, where the issues or problems which form the target for intervention are long-standing, complex or serious, more frequent meetings may be indicated.

Contact between sessions

It is not uncommon for members to contact groupworkers between sessions but how are these contacts to be handled? Are they to be accepted or refused? Will co-workers respond jointly or not? Will these contacts be recorded and reported back to the group? Will the member be asked to raise their issues in the group?

This is a difficult issue. The groupworkers may wish to appear helpful but feel they must ask the member to raise their points in the group; the member may then feel rejected, fuelling anxiety and making engaging with him or her more difficult. However, to respond may negate previous work done in the group or place the leaders in the position of not working with the group as a whole. Groupworkers need to decide for themselves and with the group their response to requests from members for contact outside the group. From the outset it should be clear whether or in what circumstances the groupworkers will respond.

It is useful to consider the meaning behind the contact. The member may have found the group experience distressing or confusing. They may have felt threatened within the group or have formed a strong dislike of some members and be considering leaving the group. Generally, it is likely that the member feels the loser in the group. Consequently, a number of questions occur. Why has this contact occurred now and how is it related to events in the group? How is this member losing out either in the group or in other contexts?

Contact should not be refused. Rather, the member should be encouraged to take responsibility for raising their issues in the group. The member may be re-experiencing difficulties in group situations or finding their significant others unsupportive of what they are trying to do. In this example, they can be invited to share these difficulties in the group, using other members for support. If the member's difficulties have a circular causation, that is the problem is located by the group within the one member but is, in fact, a problem in terms of how the group functions as a system, it may be appropriate for the groupworkers to name how the group is functioning and to challenge belief and action systems in the group without taking sides. This might be done, for instance, by asking who else might have the difficulties which this member experiences or how other members perceive that this one member experiences them or the group. Retaining neutrality is important, that is not being sucked into alliances where members can say that the workers are on their side alone.

Recording

Records have three main functions. First, to describe what has occurred in each session and the group overall. Secondly, to provide data for evaluation. Thirdly, to note significant events as a basis for discussion between the workers, for planning future sessions and for discussion with a supervisor. The recording methods adopted will vary according to the importance given to each of these functions.

The first task is to negotiate what records the agency expects and the extent to which caseworkers may have access to them. The principle of confidentiality is central to social work practice but members may expect and want information concerning them in the group to be shared with their caseworkers. Consequently, any decision concerning whether and how records are to be used outside the group should be made with group members and caseworkers.

The second task is to agree beforehand on the style to be adopted and on the purposes to which the records will be put. Thus (Hodge, 1985):

– are detailed records of each group to be kept?
– who will write the records and what is to be recorded?
– to what use will the records be put and where will they be kept?
– who may have access to the records?
– what needs to be recorded for the leaders to run the group effectively?

In the spirit of client involvement, records should be open to group members and, to counter-balance the groupworkers' perceptions, partly written by them. If records of individual members are kept, these should be open to them but the question of whether an individual's records should be open to every group member should be resolved by the group. Children's rights may be more limited but adolescents should have access to their files.

What is recorded and the techniques used will depend on the group's purposes and how the records are to be used. If the records are needed for evaluating the group, the detail required suggests that the records should be more than verbatim reports of sessions. Whatever the leaders record, it should be done immediately after each meeting when the group is still uppermost in their minds and what is recorded should be shared with the group at the beginning of the following session.

The following techniques, in all of which members can participate, may be helpful:

1. *Attendance registers*: one description of a group. If problems of attendance are noticed, what action should be taken?

2. *Sociograms*: a visual description of, for example, who talks to whom and who talks to the group or of harmony and conflict between members. Sociograms are a useful tool for evaluation. For instance, where the aim is to improve members' peer-group relationships, diagrams from several sessions will reveal the extent to which their patterns of

communication and interaction are changing or constant. Sociograms are circles with the names of members placed around the circles. Arrows to the centre indicate communication to the whole group. Arrows to individual members indicate a communication to that member. Different colours or types of arrowed lines can be used to indicate the nature of the communication.

3. *Rating scales*: useful for summarising who makes what types of contributions, who shows particular behaviours and how these develop within the group. Members can rate themselves. Ratings can be made of individual members, the categories depending on the group's purposes. Where the group aims to influence behaviour, ratings may be made of aggression with peers, withdrawn behaviour, acting out or co-operative behaviour and constructive relationships with peers and the leaders. Where the group aims to monitor roles which members adopt in the group, ratings may be made of the extent to which individual members encourage each other, agree or accept, arbitrate or share feelings, propose action or harmonise and summarise, or give and seek information and opinions (Douglas, 1976). Where the aim is to improve parent–child relationships, ratings may be made of the extent to which their interaction includes sharing feelings, clingingness, listening and play and ease of separation.

Ratings can be made of the group, the categories depending on the group's aims. The categories should be defined clearly on a scale from one (low, minimal) to five (high). The findings may suggest areas on which groupworkers should concentrate. Scales can be designed to measure the extent to which:

– there is cohesiveness in the group.
– members are supportive towards each other, co-operative or competitive.
– members exercise control.
– members participate in the group, for example in determining the group's activities.
– members use the group constructively and focus on the group's task.

4. *Sentence completion*: useful after each session or at intervals and at the close of the group for feedback from members and for evaluation. Thus:

– the worst thing about the group is . . .
– the best thing about the group is . . .
– when I come to the group I feel . . .
– the most helpful thing about the group for me is . . .
– what I enjoyed about the session(s) was . . .
– what I disliked about the session(s) was . . .
– what I found most difficult was . . .
– what I found easiest was . . .

Sentence completion can help members define goals for themselves or evaluate the impact of the group experience on their lives outside the group and define further work as a result. Thus:

– next week in the group I would like to . . .
– I have been able to use what I've got from the group by . . .
– it has been difficult for me to keep this up when . . .

5. *Tape recording*: helpful for recording key developments in the group's life, for example negotiating a contract or obtaining feedback at the mid-point or end of the group. Members' permission should be obtained and an explanation given of how the tapes will be used.

6. *Monitoring and measuring activities*: in a group which aims to help members achieve a particular skill, recording methods which involve measures of the amount or quality of a particular activity may be helpful. For example, a chart may be used to monitor the length of time a child spends on one activity.

7. *Reports*: what is included in a report of each session and the group as a whole will be influenced by who the report is for and what the groupworkers feel is relevant to their work with the group. What follows is a list of possible headings within a report:

- themes within the session.
- each member's contributions and behaviour. Are changes noticeable?
- which members were leaders, which followers? Who was scapegoated or isolated and why?
- relationships between members and between groupworkers and members.
- have sub-groups or pairings formed? What is their effect on the group?
- the climate of the group.
- agreements and decisions reached: what and how?
- ideas given by group members.
- how the group developed. Did it work well? Was everyone involved? How far have the group's goals been achieved? How fast is it progressing? What is facilitating or impeding progress?
- what changes have been made to the group's purposes? Why?
- what roles did the leaders adopt (giving direction, exercising control, stimulating or suggesting)?
- how did the co-workers interact?
- what are the groupworkers' feelings about the group?
- what is the plan for the next session or for future groupwork services?

Where reports are written after every session, periodic summaries are helpful in clarifying progress and suggesting areas on which groupworkers need to focus.

Methods

A variety of methods are available to groupworkers, from discussion to more experientially-based activities. Groupworkers may have some notion of suitable methods prior to meeting members. This may be based on models, skills and knowledge with which they are familiar, for instance analytic therapy or encounter groups, or be influenced by the type of group they envisage. Certainly the methods used must suit the leaders but they must suit the members too, be selected in consultation with them and be appropriate for the group's aims and work. To illustrate this point, some people cannot talk freely about their personal feelings or problems from fear or lack of the necessary verbal skills. In this case, a discussion group would be contra-indicated but they may benefit from a group which provides practice in other skills. In activity groups, some people may not have had an opportunity to develop skills in planning and, therefore, cannot be expected to assume responsibility for planning the group until given ideas, encouragement and assistance with their initial efforts by the leaders (Whitaker, 1975). Children are more likely to benefit from an activity group which allows discussion than from a discussion group. Finally, a group will not work where, for example, groupworkers apply a model of passive, permissive leadership and of giving interpretations to individuals or the group in a group whose members cannot participate in this type of setting.

Final decisions on the methods to be adopted can be made only after groupworkers have met the group's members. The choice of methods should relate to the needs and capabilities of members who must understand the rationale for their use. They should be oriented also towards achieving the group's stated aims which requires the leaders to consider how the group's goals might be achieved. The procedure is to discover what is required and to adopt techniques which meet these requirements. To adhere rigidly to one approach, even where the leaders favour it, might constrict the group.

Methods are not mutually exclusive but can be used in combinations. Thus, a discussion group does not need to rely exclusively on that medium for expression. Some methods are immediately obvious. Games can be used to create a therapeutic, trusting environment and to focus on group or personal development through emphasising communication, imagination, trust, confidence-building, self-disclosure and relaxation. They encourage members to share perceptions of themselves and each other, feeling cards being one method of enabling members to communicate how they perceive or are affected by others. The Gamesters' Handbook (Brandes and Philips, 1978) is a useful source book. Games such as the waiting game, rounds and brainstorming can be used for control, feedback and generating ideas. Role-play and drama gives members an experience of what it is like to be someone else and can be used, for example in groups concentrating on developing social skills, to practise behaviours or to drama- tise problems or difficulties experienced by members. These experiences can open up discussion. They are a useful tech- nique for providing members with understanding of their behaviour, their relationships, feelings and attitudes towards others, and how others react to them. Movement can be used to develop skills in expressing emotions and in non- verbal communication and to improve relationships between members. For example, dance and movement can be used to improve the bonding between parents and toddlers. A group may engage in work tasks such as the organisation of jumble sales or petitions, both to achieve social change goals and to foster individual development. Finally, groups may use dis- cussion, either centred around topics introduced by the members or groupworkers, or free-floating. Groupworkers may find that the group works quicker and is less anxiety- provoking if they introduce topics but this might not be appropriate always for the group's aims. If co-workers have different ideas about methods, this can disrupt the environ- ment which they are seeking to create to foster the group's work and result in one becoming uninvolved.

However, I believe that groupworkers should look further afield for methods. The structural and systemic schools of family therapy use a variety of methods which can assist group members to understand the dynamics of and their contribution to the group. Two techniques especially appear useful. Sculpting is a useful tool for demonstrating the emotional positions that members put each other in, a physical portrayal of how one member sees people's posi- tions and attitudes towards each other. In a group it may enhance the perceptions of conflicts in a group. It may build up members' skills by sculpting their perception of the group so that they can see how it feels to be fixed in a position into which they place others. It may enhance the supportive potential of a group by building up care skills through their perception of relationships within the group and is a method of plotting the pattern of interpersonal relationships within the group, indicating the changes members perceive as desirable and the path to be travelled to attain them (Hopkins, 1981). Sculpting enables members to be aware of feelings about one another which, otherwise, they might be unable to acknowledge or verbalise. It can elicit impressions of the group's structure and may free and focus communication, making explicit implicit relationships, roles, mutual perceptions and expectations. It provides information on the group's structure and behaviour which may stimulate discussion on changes which would facilitate the group's functioning.

The second technique is circular questioning (Selvini *et al.*, 1980; Penn, 1982). This involves avoiding blaming and attributions of madness or badness and maintaining neutrality, that is not siding with one against another. Information is collected about views of the problem, the group's beliefs and organisation, by encouraging members to verbalise what they believe other members and people outside the group would say. Circular questioning explores differences, particularly changes in relationships around significant events, and elicits ratings and rankings of behaviour, feelings and interactions by asking one person to comment on a dyadic relationship in the group or on what another member might say about them or the group. It aims to perceive differences and change, for example before and after an event, on the basis that differences are information.

Leadership styles and roles

The final preliminary before the first session in terms of the group's operation, once specific aims and a programme have been devised, is to consider what style of leadership to use, what roles to adopt. Groupworkers bring to a group expertise in particular areas or clear preferences of style. This may lead them to determine the roles they will adopt prior to receiving referrals, perhaps modifying them in the process of engaging with the group and assessing the members' resources. I believe that to develop fixed ideas about roles too early, perhaps out of a need for security, is inadvisable since the plan may be inappropriate or fail to take account of the evolution of the group or co-work partnership. In any case, decisions about roles made at the outset of the group will require modification in the course of the group to reflect its developments, members' emerging needs and the increasing confidence and emerging skills of members and leaders alike. For instance, groupworkers initially may assume responsibility for determining the activities for each session. However, members may develop their skills such that responsibility can be passed to them.

Groupworkers can adopt a variety of roles. Clarity of role is important for effective groupwork and leader satisfaction. Without it, their interventions in the group will be muddled and uncertain, confusing and counter-productive for members. A useful initial question is whether leadership is to be shared or co-workers to function on the basis of a leader and assistant. It is either to be the 'senior' in meetings? Where students or volunteers are working with more experienced groupworkers, roles may be divided initially on the basis of the experienced worker being a facilitator and guide with the student or volunteer an assistant, present to learn as much as to contribute. However, the confidence of the less experienced leaders may increase and after several sessions they may feel able to take a more active role. Accordingly, it is useful to assess continually the needs, development and wishes of the participants and to revise role relationships when this seems indicated.

Where leadership is to be shared on the basis of shared roles and equal status, it is useful to recall that equal status must account for differences in style and experience, and that shared roles does not mean necessarily that all the roles are undertaken equally. There are a variety of possible roles (Dowling, 1979) including:

- introducing tasks, opening and concluding sessions.
- proposing: putting forward a new concept, suggestion or course of action.
- building: extending or developing the actions, proposals, comments or contributions of oneself or another.
- supporting: giving support or agreement to another person.
- disagreeing: declaring a difference of opinion or criticising another.

- open: self-exposure, disclosing personal experiences or feelings.
- testing understanding: whether a contribution has been understood. Testing consensus.
- integrating: summarising the discussion or content. Clarifying.
- eliciting: seeking information, opinions or clarification.
- giving information and opinions.
- bringing in: involving a member.
- challenging: a behaviour to provoke expression of feelings.
- enlarging: expanding the meaning of contributions by interpreting or providing awareness of underlying dimensions.
- pointing out: highlighting another's behaviour which has not been commented upon.
- encouraging and maintaining the group task.
- observation of the group's process.
- harmonising, bringing about compromise.
- discouraging or reinforcing behaviour.
- verbalising the group's concerns.

One leader may be more supportive and nurturing, the other more challenging and inclined to confrontation; one passive, one active. Or, the leaders may take turns to observe the group. Specialist knowledge or preference for a particular style may mean that one leader takes charge of particular areas of the group's activities or process (Hodge, 1985). Accordingly, before the group:

- who will assume responsibility for task issues in the group (achieving goals; giving and seeking information and opinion; initiating; summarising) and who will address themselves to the process interactions within and the emotional atmosphere of the group (group maintenance skills of observing processes; resolving conflicts; building trust; evaluating the emotional climate)? These responsibilities may be shared or divided out.
- who will focus on issues within the group and who on events outside it but affecting its dynamics? These tasks may be shared or divided out.

- who will open and close sessions? Who will liaise with colleagues?
- how do the leaders propose to engage members and how are difficulties in the group, for example of control, to be handled? What difficulties may arise and how might these be avoided or managed?
- what do the leaders believe are the tasks and responsibilities of groupworkers? What leadership styles are congenial to them and within their competence and are these styles appropriate for the group?

Some groupworkers have a directive approach, preferring to be central to the group's organisation and running. Others prefer to be more permissive and non-directive. Some prefer a high level of self-disclosure, others the reverse. Some have expertise in interpreting processes. Groupworkers need to consider whether their preferences and expertise in terms of style is appropriate for the group and, where co-working, to ensure that a mutually acceptable approach is possible. Where roles are divided out, some flexibility is necessary so that each may intervene when they feel it appropriate.

Factors external to the group

Groups do not exist in isolation from their environment. Indeed, many founder because their base is not established securely within wider systems. Thus, it is as important that groupworkers concentrate on the environment in which they are practising as it is to focus on the group's structure and operation. Indeed, environmental factors can undermine a well-planned group which is why referral forms and offering the group should take account of the attitudes of significant members of the client's family and environment.

Significant others

The co-operation of significant others outside the group is important. Just as for effective groupwork the leaders will be helped by a co-operative stance from their colleagues and agency, so too for members. Their aims and membership may be frustrated by hostility, indifference or incomprehension within their families and extended networks. Therefore, it is useful to consider what the attitudes of significant others will be to members joining the group and whether some work needs to be directed at these systems prior to the beginning of the group. This could include explaining the group's purpose, stressing the importance of regular attendance and the undesirability of parents using non-attendance as a punishment for children.

Agency considerations

Groupworkers should not take for granted the co-operation of colleagues since, crucial to the group's success, they may prove unhelpful, obstructive, ambivalent, defensive or uninterested. They may see groupwork as a threat to established ways of working and feel that their abilities and sense of security as caseworkers are threatened. Since casework is the prevalent intervention method in most organisations and since many practitioners prefer to work with individuals or families, they may be unconvinced of groupwork's value or unresponsive to new ideas. Many supervisors are inexperienced in supervising groupwork. This absence of support can weaken groupworkers' confidence and motivation or increase their isolation and anxieties. Groupwork may take place too in a climate of limited resources where groupworkers have to compete for resources and convince colleagues of the need for and viability of a group.

Practitioners may respond to this situation by refraining from being too specific about their aims for the group or criteria for membership both to ensure that clients are referred and to minimise the risk of opposition or observed failure (Adams, 1984). Another is to begin the group with inadequate resources in terms of money, rooms and transport.

To overcome these reactions, it is good practice to present a proposal to colleagues, to invite comment and to discuss the resources needed for the group and the implications of this for the agency's overall commitments. Groupworkers should try to anticipate potential difficulties and encourage both the expression of reservations and how colleagues view the leaders and the group. The team should aim for a consensus about the place of groupwork and any particular group in their setting (Sturton, 1972; Whitaker, 1975). In this the groupworkers may have some or each of the following roles. First, as change agents in respect of their agency, to modify attitudes by theoretical argument or by demonstrating groupwork's usefulness. Secondly, modifying their aims to enlist support. Thirdly, considering whether to discuss with the group the agency's attitudes and to examine whether the group has a task in engaging with the agency in a dialogue about its attitudes and the services it provides.

The support of the agency can make a substantial, either negative or positive, contribution. Therefore, groupworkers should be aware of whom they need to consult and inform, what authority they have in the group delegated by the agency and how the group might contribute to the overall service being offered by the agency. Thus:

- how is the group to be explained to members, their families and those clients who are not included?
- what liaison is necessary with those who have or might refer people to the group and what feedback will be given to them?
- will co-workers do this jointly or separately?
- is one leader responsible for co-ordinating the project?
- to whom are the leaders accountable and for what?
- whose authority and support is required?
- who needs to be informed and consulted?

Conclusion

This section has outlined what can make the difference between an effective and ineffective group. Whether or not a group materialises will depend largely on the care and time taken over planning. The main factor responsible for ineffectiveness is the lack of adequate preparation.

One final area remains to be discussed before workers meet with the group in the first session. This is the decision relating to co-work or single leadership and preparing themselves for the group. This is discussed in the next two chapters.

4

Co-leadership

Introduction

When planning a group, practitioners have a choice between solo and co-leadership. Despite its widespread prevalence, co-work is not necessarily appropriate with all groups. In groups relying primarily on discussion, one worker may be the most appropriate since members may feel outnumbered, threatened or intimidated by the presence of co-leaders. Two workers may prove too top-heavy in a small group but may be useful in activity groups in monitoring and controlling the group. However, co-workers may not prevent disruptive or destructive activity or help to control the group. Using three or more workers can create both confusion regarding the structure of and roles in leadership and a situation where leaders and members form and co-exist as sub-groups.

There must be clear reasons, therefore, for using more than one leader, based on the nature of the group and practitioners' preferences. The first part of this chapter discusses the advantages and contra-indicators of co-leadership and the relevance of the type of group and practitioners' personal views for the choice of modality. The second part of the chapter will outline the factors which contribute to the establishment of a successful co-work relationship.

Co-leadership: why and when?

Much co-work seems inspired by a reluctance to lead a group alone and by the advantages which co-work is seen to convey (Preston-Shoot, 1986). However, co-leadership has been neglected in groupwork literature. I believe that the discrepancy between literature and practice reflects an off-the-peg, practice-wisdom approach (Douglas, 1982) where practitioners' use of co-leadership is based more on their preference for this modality than on what is required for the group.

Where groupwork literature has considered co-leadership, usually it describes its potential advantages. However, these advantages do not emerge automatically and, in my experience, practitioners do not use co-work selectively but see it as necessary and effective for all groups (Preston-Shoot, 1986). This view, that co-leadership is the best and indeed only method of leading groups, seems based on the perceived advantages of co-working, groupworkers' personal needs and those of group members. I wish to encourage groupworkers to move away from a trend of considering that every group benefits from two workers towards questioning whether co-leadership is appropriate. Therefore, I shall discuss two sets of factors, both of which should be considered when choosing the leadership modality: the nature of the group and the resources and preferences which groupworkers bring to their task.

The nature of the group

Size

Brown (1979) argues that the larger the group, the more co-work is indicated, presumably for the purposes of control, monitoring interactions and maintaining tasks. This view is too simplistic. Many small groups are co-led (Preston-Shoot, 1986) and co-work in large groups may be contra-indicated. Rather than size per se, the appropriate leadership modality may become apparent from considering these questions:

- given the group's objectives, would two workers be super-fluous in the group?
- will group members be threatened, intimidated or over-whelmed by co-workers?
- would one worker feel overwhelmed or find controlling and containing the group difficult?
- will there be a lot of activity to monitor and manage such that co-leaders could cope more effectively with the volume and complexity of the group's material?
- is more than one view about what is happening in the group or evaluation of group dynamics important? Is it intended that significant events such as scapegoating or rivalry for leadership should be observed and fed-back to the group? Is it felt that this would be easier with a co-worker?
- where the centrality of the workers for the group is to be de-emphasised, will leaders emerge more easily from within the group if there is only one leader?

Continuity

Where it is important that the continuity of the group is not disrupted, co-leadership does enable sessions to continue when one leader is absent. However, it may not be necessary for leaders to be present for the group to meet and the absence of one leader can be just as disruptive of continuity as no session at all. Therefore, how important is continuity in the group and, if important, how best might it be maintained?

Type of member

Brown (1979) states that the more problematic the group, the more co-work is indicated. This is too simplistic. A single leader may be able to formulate effective strategies for preventing or responding to difficulties such as hostility or controlling the group. Nor does it follow necessarily that, where members are very demanding, co-working will prevent or make it easier to deal with problems of disruption or dependent behaviour. This is because members may react negatively to what they see as an excessive presence of power and authority in the group (Whitaker, 1985).

Where one result of the group might be the expression of strong feelings or demands for individual attention, co-work may enable the leaders to work more effectively. For example, a single leader may feel uncertain about encouraging the expression of powerful emotions or, where attention has to be given to one or several members, a co-worker can enable the remainder of the group to continue working without loss of direction. Where it is anticipated that there may be problems of containment or involving members in the group's tasks, co-work may be indicated provided that the leaders have an agreed strategy and feel that the group is more likely to consider two leaders more seriously than one.

Aims and purposes

Co-leadership is indicated where the aims and purposes of the group include:

– work in sub-groups. Co-workers can link the work of sub-groups and indicate the complementary part each holds for the other, the similarities and differences.
– providing members with an opportunity to experience themselves with the interest, concern, involvement and authority of different people.
– modelling social, communication and interactional skills (Hodge, 1985) and exposing the group to a functional relationship which can be used as a model (Dowling, 1979).

Co-work may enable members to experience a co-operative, creative relationship based on collaboration, trust, clear communication and the expression and resolution of disagreements without threatening self-esteem. Where co-workers are of opposite gender, this provides the group with a valuable experience of a partnership working collaboratively with mutual respect without destructive competition, mutual derogation, exploitation or pervasive sexuality

(Yalom, 1970). Modelling aims to show members not simply what to do within or outside the group, but to enable them to find healthier ways of meeting their needs. The model provides the group with the opportunity to make overt disagreements within it, to work through feelings about authority figures, and to experience discomfort without permanent harm. It may counteract stereotyping by providing an experience of learning to differentiate others according to their individual attributes rather than their gender roles (Douglas, 1976; Zaro *et al.*, 1977; Muir, 1978; Brown *et al.*, 1982).

It seems that co-working is contra-indicated where one worker is coping well already. It is inappropriate also where practitioners hold widely divergent goals, styles and expertise since this can create uncertainty, miscommunication or lack of clarity in the group and will make it difficult for the leaders to work well together.

The decision is less clear-cut in groups where the aim is to encourage members to express their views to social workers, having the support of other members, and where the purpose is to enable members to assume responsibility for the direction, structure and programme of the group. In such examples, the questions which must be asked are:

- will the leaders find it easier to pursue these aims alone or with a colleague?
- what is the likely outcome for the leaders and members if solo or co-leadership is adopted?
- will the members find it easier to use the group for the set purposes if there is one leader?
- what skills are necessary for the practitioners to possess for this group and would one leader have the resources required?

Where there is a wide range of activities and material or in groups where the emphasis is not only on the accomplishment of tasks but also on monitoring, observing and commenting on the group's process, co-leadership offers several advantages. It reduces the pressures and stress on groupworkers since leaders do not have to be active throughout or feel that they have to possess all the skills and knowledge necessary. Leadership tasks can be shared to respond to the group's tasks and dynamics and to utilise practitioners' different strengths, thereby increasing the skills and methods available to the group. Co-workers can share or accept total responsibility for monitoring the group's process, that is individual and group behaviour, and recording events as they occur or for initiating tasks with the group and attending to members' individual needs, feelings and behaviour (Hodge, 1985). Co-work may enable leaders to achieve an easier balance between challenge or criticism and support (Piggin and Watson, 1979) and to reinforce each other's contributions in the group. In demanding groups it may assist practitioners in avoiding comfortable sessions where there is empathy but no impact, and in expressing their concerns to the group.

Groupworkers' resources and preferences

Various non-group related factors influence practitioners towards co-leadership. Their training in groupwork may have been minimal. Social workers often feel that their training did not reflect the practice skills required within an agency or prepare them for groupwork (Davies, 1984). This may leave groupworkers aware of the problems and complexities but uncertain of their skills in handling them. Alongside this is mistrust, ambivalence, even fear about groups which seem more demanding than casework. Agency norms may dictate the use of co-leadership or practitioners may adopt it to argue for their group more forcefully or to cope with discouraging events and the fear of failure within their work setting. Establishing a group can be a struggle, especially where groupwork is not an established, accepted method of working within an agency, and leaders may have to work hard to achieve discussion and acceptance of their group. Finally, a common feature is a lack of confidence. This is partly because social workers have difficulty in recognising the relevance of previous groupwork and social work experience and in identifying the knowledge, skills and theoretical frameworks which they hold. All these factors may suggest that co-work is indicated.

Groupworkers can expect a number of potential gains from co-leadership, namely:

- a source of support, comfort and feedback. The shared responsibility for the group increases the likelihood of thoroughness and helps workers who feel stuck or at a loss (Douglas, 1976; Muir, 1978; Dick *et al.*, 1980; Whitaker, 1985).
- a means of overcoming limited personal skills, fears about personal capabilities and competence, and of building confidence through sharing responsibility and learning from another worker's style and experience (Zaro *et al.*, 1977).
- a forum for learning about oneself, one's style of inter-action in groups (McGee and Schuman, 1970) or for professional growth from working through a relationship with a colleague (Yalom, 1970).
- security and protection, enhanced pleasure and satisfac-tion (Dowling, 1979). Co-work offers mutual support, someone who has experienced the group to talk to after-wards. Co-workers can clarify each other's contributions and challenge or compensate for any feelings that each may have of limited skills and competence. The support may encourage groupworkers to be more adventurous in the group, having a colleague for guidance on whether an intervention is appropriate and at times of stress. Quite simply, co-work can enhance their ability to cope (Muir, 1978).
- training opportunities for a less-experienced worker (Hodge, 1985).
- the leadership resources in planning, keeping focus and responding to a group's many events and needs are en-riched (Douglas, 1976; Hodge, 1985). Co-leadership in-creases the range of options, techniques and styles available to the group and, therefore, the likelihood that the group's needs will be understood and met.

However, if this personal dimension frees practitioners to obtain the maximum advantages from working in a group, these gains are justified only if there are advantages also for the group. The implied advantage for the group is that the leaders' work will be more productive, that if the workers feel more comfortable co-working, there are likely to be spin-offs for the group providing co-work is not contra-indicated by the nature and needs of the group. There is a danger that, once co-working has been experienced, the tendency to use this method is reinforced, irrespective of training and experience, because groupworkers are reluctant to lead a group alone and find in co-leadership a safe haven (Breslin and Sturton, 1974; Walrond-Skinner, 1976). This is because practitioners lack confidence and feel that solo leadership does not offer them an opportunity to develop their groupwork skills more fully (Preston-Shoot, 1986). In order that practitioners can consider the nature of the group more fully when determining which leadership modality to use, they should be enabled to identify and evaluate the impact of groupworking on their skills and resources and to consider whether these are adequate for the task. In the next chapter some guidelines are offered on how this might be done through answering questions like:

– what personal goals are they setting for themselves?
– what are they hoping to learn through co-leadership?
– what skills and resources do they have?
– what have they learned?

When to begin planning with a co-worker?

Planning a group with a co-worker preferably should begin before either worker individually has given any detailed consideration to the group. This view is based on the belief that the further the planning stage has reached prior to the introduction of a co-worker, the more difficult it will be for the original worker to relinquish total control of the work and for the incoming leader to feel that the project is a shared endeavour in which they are able to make their contribution and develop their skills and ideas. This is true especially for leaders who join a group because a previous groupworker has left. In this circumstance, the groupwork-ers should establish first of all a sound relationship and secondly review the group's aims. This is to ensure that the contribution of the incoming worker can be accommodated and that differences of opinion concerning aims, methods or goals will not interfere with the group's functioning. Conflict is possible unless the newcomer is given time in preparation to discuss their thoughts and feelings about the group and allowed to influence previously made decisions (Hodge, 1985).

Many of the questions raised above, the answers to which indicate the appropriateness or otherwise of co-leadership, cannot be answered without knowledge of the group's membership and purposes. This may not be available at the outset. Accordingly, the appropriateness or otherwise of co-leadership should be kept under review as planning proceeds and the details of the nature of the group and the resources of the individual groupworkers become clearer.

Selecting a co-worker

Having decided on co-leadership, what qualities are necessary for an effective, viable partnership? How may compatibility or suitability be defined? To what extent should groupworkers, in their choice of co-worker, reflect the composition or meet the needs of the group? How far should they be influenced by considerations of their mutual compatibility, personal interests or their combined usefulness for the group?

One study of factors crucial for successful co-working identified three essential components, namely:

– practitioners' theoretical orientation and beliefs.
– ways of handling and identifying problems in terms of practitioners' style and skills.
– quality and quantity of practitioners' participation : agreement on how active or inactive the leaders should be (Paulson *et al.*, 1976).

The intention here is to move beyond the statement that co-work is inappropriate where potential colleagues cannot work well together or feel so uncomfortable that effective communication and work is unlikely (Piggin and Watson,

1979) towards identifying those factors which are essential ingredients for a successful partnership. To some extent, choice will be idiosyncratic, dependent on the workers doing the choosing, in the sense that they will be influenced by their self-perceptions and understanding of their own needs and resources. Therefore, groupworkers should be clear on what matters to them, on who is likely to be a resource for themselves and why this might be so. However, it is possible to define factors necessary for an effective partnership.

Shared values, philosophy and theoretical orientation

Co-work is inappropriate where the workers hold very divergent theoretical stances or personal styles (Piggin and Watson, 1979) because disagreements and differences will reduce the effectiveness of their interventions and confuse the group and their understanding of its dynamics. A high level of commitment to groupwork is required, a belief in groupwork as a method of intervention, both to sustain their involvement with a group and to engage the agency in the project. This is a commitment to 'thinking groups' as well as identifying the grounds for justifying groupwork as a method of intervention generally and in respect of the proposed membership. Accordingly, potential co-workers should discuss their philosophical and theoretical orientations, their similarities and differences prior to committing themselves to co-leadership.

Co-workers require similar views, common working values and similar basic assumptions and professional outlooks to be able to work together. For example, social workers planning a women's group should share similar views and values regarding women's issues. Again, if co-workers hold different beliefs about the rights of members to determine or change the group's task or about the causes of members' difficulties, such as offending, these differences may make it difficult for practitioners to enable the group to work effectively or to devise a programme which feels satisfactory to the members. Moreover, these similarities might not be apparent immediately. Preparatory work will be necessary to ensure that co-leaders share basic attitudes and a compatible method of working. This involves testing out with each other their beliefs about the nature and causes of members' problems and the compatibility of their groupwork practice principles and theoretical orientation (Hodge, 1985). It involves identifying the influences on their thinking about groupwork and their theoretical approach and preferred ways of working, for example: psychodynamic, discussion and members selecting the topics for focus. This is not to suggest that co-leaders should share identical interests, beliefs or values but that their views on the aims of the group, how these are to be achieved and how they will lead the group should be sufficiently compatible for them to work together effectively (Hodge, 1985).

Shared aims for the group

Whitaker (1985) refers to the importance of compatible stances to the group. She means by this that co-leaders should feel congenial in and share similar views about their approach to the group, what they hope the group can accomplish and how they will function within the group setting. Compatible attitudes are necessary towards the variety of problems and situations which may emerge in the group. A clash of perspectives and a failure to examine inevitable points of conflict or develop a consensus on aims and procedures for a group will result in the group and the leaders having difficulty in understanding its development and in beginning work.

Therefore, at the outset, co-workers should establish whether they hold similar views about how to run the group and the techniques or skills required for it. Ideas about the group, what the work is about, and on aims and expectations for the group need to be broadly similar. This stress on common ground is very necessary. Whether informed by theoretical models and/or practice experience, workers require a rationale in order to pursue a task effectively, a framework within which to conduct the group. In social work generally it is essential for both clients and workers to share a belief in a rationale which encompasses both an explanation of the problems being tackled and of the methods to be used. Groupwork is no exception. Both leaders and members need to believe that the theoretical propositions underpinning the group and the related practical methods to be used are beneficial. I am not suggesting that all ambiguity, uncertainty and disagreement should be excluded but that the commitment to co-working requires a compatible outlook in respect of social work generally and the group in particular and that disagreements are contra-indicators unless the leaders are sure that a compromise is workable (Hodge, 1985).

Beyond a shared interest in the work and type of group proposed, some groupworkers may find that a personal interest in working with the client group is central. However, the absence of an interest in a particular group of clients is not necessarily a contra-indicator. For instance, students often are allocated to a group. In my experience, where difficulties have arisen in their co-working, these have related not so much to an absence of interest in the client group as to difficulties involved in inheriting an already established brief, finding space for their contribution and roles of benefit to the group and co-work partnership. In my opinion, the distinction between starting from scratch and joining an established project is most important. The latter is a much more difficult undertaking, requiring considerable sensitivity and openness by both co-workers.

Professional skills

Since co-work and groupwork are demanding both personally and professionally, co-workers must feel confident with each other. Otherwise, it may prove difficult to use the advantages that co-leadership offers, particularly in terms of modelling, and the co-workers may be more vulnerable to splitting by the group's members. Several qualities appear significant here. First, an ability to keep to the aims of the group and to challenge and work without feeling threatened within the partnership. Secondly, a belief that colleagues can manage the group experience confidently and competently and are able to take the initiative. Thirdly, since groupwork-ers may lack confidence in their skills or be hoping to learn from a co-worker, a willingness to identify what skills are required for the work and owned by the workers. This enables the groupworkers to be clear about whether they have the skills appropriate to particular parts of the group and whether a colleague has the skills with which their partner does not feel comfortable.

Attitudes to co-work

Co-leaders should be prepared to devote time to developing the co-work partnership. They should be willing to give and accept constructive feedback and have an attitude of openness and honesty in resolving conflict, in sorting out and working at the group's aims, and in discussing difficulties encountered in preparation for and in leading the group. They should be prepared to disclose their thoughts and feelings relating to the problems or circumstances addressed by the group so as not to offer members or each other misleading signals based on separate sets of premises concerning what the issues or problems are about (Hodge, 1985).

Any co-work relationship will encounter stress, conflict and differences. Co-workers will be tested out by the group and the stress or tension which can be created by groupwork makes them susceptible to conflict (Hodge, 1985). If the strength and stability of the dyad is to be promoted, a com-mitment is needed to an honest, critical appreciation of both partners' work, of what they feel about each other's ways of working. They should feel able to communicate clearly and resolve problems without experiencing negative reper-cussions from each other. Both in preparation and when leading the group, leaders must be prepared to review how they are working together and to tackle any differences of opinion. Otherwise they may become distant from each other and lose awareness of how group processes are influen-cing them (Hodge, 1985). For example, they may believe that their partner is creating difficulties rather than locate them within the group itself or within the systems which impinge on it such as the attitudes of the agency and the level of resources or support it provides. The rationale for discussing the feelings which co-leadership and the group bring to the fore is that the capacity of the group to deal with its tasks and tensions is related directly to the ability of the co-leaders to discuss their own interpersonal tensions and differences of opinion (Hodge, 1977). For instance, a reluctance to mention what leaders find irritating about each other, in order to avoid the fear of a rift in the partnership, may signal to the group that expressing disagreements and differences harms relationships and members may be wary of exploring what is happening within the group.

Personal response to a potential colleague

A common anxiety when beginning co-work, however experienced the groupworkers, is the fear of not being good enough, a self-assessment of limited experience and confidence. Co-working is likely to be a rewarding experience where colleagues are comfortable to be with and engender feelings of self-worth, confidence and respect for each others' skills. Helpful too is a willingness to engage in identifying and developing the strengths and resources they already have. Put another way, co-leadership is more fruitful when the partners are prepared to participate in each other's changes, to confront their own blind-spots and to accept and integrate their own and their colleague's skills into the partnership.

Similarity or dissimilarity: Homogeneity or heterogeneity?

Piggin and Watson (1979) express the view that a partnership is appropriate when workers have complementary skills suitable for the proposed task. For them, co-working is inappropriate where differences in experience are such that one leader is likely to feel inhibited and where their gender combination is unsuitable for the group. This raises the questions of the styles of the potential co-leaders, of gender

combinations and of the professional status of the participants. Once again, some consideration is necessary of the
advantages and complications surrounding similarity.

A successful combination is one in which there is similarity in terms of a shared ethos about social work, groups
and the aims for the particular group in question, together
with some dissimilarity in terms of the skills and strengths
brought to the group by the two leaders. In other words,
where the basic goals are shared but where workers offer
different skills and emphases to the common aims. Some
differences in personality are desirable too, for example
between directiveness/interventionist and passive/observation,
but not so extreme that one leader's contribution will smother
the other's.

The emphasis is on complementarity. Similar styles and
strengths can result in omissions and deficits in technique
and in avoidance of particular issues both within the partnership and the group. The areas and issues which may be
explored in the group are reduced and effectiveness is limited. For example, where co-leaders work at similar levels of
intensity, this may make their detachment from the group
process difficult. Where the leaders are 'over-united', members may have difficulty in making an impact on them.
Equally, however, having too-divergent qualities can create
difficulties in communication and leading the group coher-
ently. The most effective partnership is one where there is
differentiation, where the partners are clearly different persons, with different strengths, but with a shared basic stance
and values relating to the group (Whitaker, 1985). This
differentiation should provide a healthy model of interaction
and functioning for the group and help to dispel any myths
that disagreements and differences are unhelpful.

Style

Worker style is a major influence on social worker functioning (Brown, 1977). Accordingly, an explicit definition of
style should be used as a basis for allocating tasks. Further,
identifying worker style can have an impact on cohesiveness,
trust and sharing and on the optimum deployment of re-

sources. It can free practitioners from the feeling of being expected to be competent in all tasks and enable them to concentrate on those skills and methods congruent with their style. Brown's analysis is very applicable to co-working groups. The use of co-leaders enables roles and tasks to be distributed. Where the styles brought by co-leaders are too similar or divergent, the effective distribution of functions within the group may be difficult. Complementary styles offer the chance of a greater degree of diversity and potential richness for the group. Therefore, groupworkers need to understand their partner's style of work and preparation should include focussing on how workers practice in groups and their possible contribution to the group.

Gender combinations

A male/female team may provide a balanced, effective model and opportunity for the group to work through misconceptions and fantasies concerning the leaders' relationship. It provides members with the possibility of experiencing a functional, mixed relationship. However, similar opportunities may be available through a single gender partnership.

This issue should be decided by three questions. First, what is the right gender combination for the group? Two male workers working with an all-female membership may find the absence of a female worker a disadvantage. A male/female partnership may be indicated when working with a membership comprising of partners and examining relationship difficulties. Secondly, what are the personal preferences of the workers and are these compatible with the gender combination suggested by the group's composition? Thirdly, what preparation is necessary to ensure the viability of the partnership?

The professional status of the co-workers

A partnership is inappropriate where differences in experience or status are so great that one leader feels inhibited

(Piggin and Watson, 1979). Where students or newcomers are introduced to groupwork with a more experienced co-leader, initially they may have little confidence in themselves as partners. They may be concerned about how they will be perceived by members or colleagues. They may experience difficulty in achieving a satisfying role or in developing their own skills. The more experienced groupworker may feel that the relationship lacks balance by virtue of their having more experience and greater confidence in the group. The inexperienced worker may collude with an uneven distribution of tasks. Group members may become aware of the differences in skill and authority and relate or respond to the experienced groupworker. However, with adequate preparation and regular reviews of the development of their skills and confidence, this pairing may present a useful introduction to groupwork for the inexperienced practitioner provided that they are allowed to develop their styles and techniques and are encouraged to take an active part in the sessions.

Where one leader holds a senior position within the agency, even where the co-worker is the more experienced groupworker, acting as co-equals can be difficult both because of the positional agency authority of the 'senior' and because members may invest the 'senior' with more authority. This circumstance may arise too where leaders are drawn from different professions where inter-professional and public perceptions of status may result in members and leaders according more authority to one professional, for example a medic, even if that professional is the less experienced groupworker. These circumstances can unsettle a co-work relationship. However, their effectiveness should not be affected if they have thought through this situation and have a clear, agreed understanding of their roles in the group (Hodge, 1985), how these differ from roles and positions in respect of authority and decision-making which they hold in their setting, and how to present this to the group. Otherwise, tensions may break into and be played out in the group and co-work relationship. Specifically, they should clarify which of them is responsible for the various tasks relating to the group and whether authority generally and final decision-making authority is shared or assumed by one of them. Where authority is placed in one leader, the nature of the authority should be clarified. For example, does it include who should be admitted into the group (Hodge, 1985)?

How to present co-work to the group

Frequently the question of explaining the presence of co-workers in a group is neglected. Just as the workers' predominant experience will be one-to-one work, so may clients be uncertain, suspicious or puzzled by the use of two leaders. Members may question their presence or react by showing a preference for one leader based on a perception of differences in status or on the roles adopted by the group-workers in the group. Alternatively, they may attempt to split the partnership and undermine the relationship, especially if they feel intimidated by the presence of more than one leader. If these dynamics are not discussed by the co-workers, they may find themselves in competition for or colluding with the attention of the members. These reactions can take energy away from the group's tasks. If an explanation for the use of co-workers is not given, this assumes members' understanding and co-operation which social work often takes for granted. Further, it prevents group-workers from discussing with the group this part of its dynamics and how this changes over time.

In the spirit of client involvement, I believe that group-workers should decide how to explain the presence of co-workers to the group and discuss in the group how members perceive the leaders and what their fantasies might be concerning the presence of co-workers. A simple and truthful explanation at the outset is good practice, for example that two workers offer different perceptions, experience and skills for the group and can ensure that the many events in a group are not missed.

Conclusion

In this chapter I have discussed factors which may suggest that co-leadership is an appropriate leadership modality and which form the basis for an effective partnership. In both instances, the choice should be influenced by considerations of the composition, needs and purposes of the group, the workers' compatibility and their combined usefulness for the group. It will be apparent that friendship and availability alone are insufficient indicators for a co-work partnership. Well prepared co-work can be an effective, economic use of resources. Preparation is crucial if co-leadership is to produce the gains expected of it. A further rationale for preparation is that it enables the leaders to prepare for the complexities of groupwork and co-work which, otherwise, can preoccupy members, disrupt communication and divert energy away from the groupwork. Methods of preparation are discussed in the next chapter.

5

Preparation for Leading a Group

Introduction

This chapter has two purposes. First, to identify why preparation for leadership is essential for effective groupwork and to outline how this may be done. Secondly, to provide a framework in which practitioners can place their developing confidence and skills in groupwork. This framework is offered because each new experience takes social workers into both familiar and unchartered territory. Previous assumed mastery may feel questionable or the demands of a new situation may fit uneasily with old routines. The new task may lead to or be part of a more fundamental questioning of previously held beliefs and values and will provoke hopes and preoccupations. The skills and expertise, once confidently taken for granted, may be thrown into question to such an extent that groupworkers may be unable to practise as confidently as they had been accustomed to. Indeed, groupworkers may find it difficult to identify the skills, knowledge and experience they are bringing to and their relevance for the task.

Why prepare for co-leadership?

Why is it essential for co-leaders to consider whether and how they can work together effectively? One answer lies within the dynamics and potential of the co-work relationship. A creative relationship, based on trust and collaboration, does not emerge immediately. Time is needed for the leaders to understand each other's thoughts and feelings about the group and their ways of handling situations in a group, and to develop an inner security in relation to the group so that neither will be dependent unduly on the other for support in the face of group pressures (Hodge, 1985). Nor will the ability to evaluate critically their working together necessarily be present from the outset. Time has to be devoted to allow trust to develop from which the co-workers may feel secure enough to confront each other, to express their feelings and views and to use their skills, strengths and differences to attain an effective working relationship. As with any relationship, the possibility exists for the development of conflict or destructive patterns of inter-relationship. These may have their roots in differences in perception or expectations and in private conceptualisations of the proposed group or co-work pairing and of events within them. Co-workers may present their relationship as characterised by complete agreement and the absence of conflict and differences. In all probability this reflects a false organisation. It may suggest to both group members and co-workers that it is unsafe to express disagreement or create an atmosphere where the dominant assumption is that conflict is inimical to the group's task and the development of co-working. An uncomfortable partnership may arise from competitiveness and rivalry or where there is a wide divergence of styles and opinions. These possible patterns can inhibit effective work if they remain unresolved or latent, available to be stirred up by and played out in the group experience. Preparation, then, can help the co-leaders avoid working against each other.

A second answer lies in the way a potential co-work partnership may arise. It may result from previous experience of working together or follow from discussion. Alternatively, team members or an individual staff member may propose a particular pairing. Equally possible is an absence of choice.

Where choice is restricted, co-workers may feel pressurised into ensuring that the partnership proves viable, both to ensure a successful group and, where students are involved, a satisfactory outcome to the placement. These pressures can lead the participants to minimise differences of opinion or anxieties concerning their abilities to the detriment of the group. They may conceal personality clashes or neither express nor explore their expectations of each other and of the modality. They may assume that their styles of working are compatible. In such circumstances there is an increased likelihood that the co-leaders will be disappointed and their effectiveness reduced.

Even where choice is based on prior acquaintance or previous experience of working together, an immediate decision to work together is inadvisable. Knowledge and assumptions, gained from one context, may not be applicable in another situation, or beneficial for the task of leading a group. If the pairing is formed because of prior acquaintance or friendship, it is important to ensure that the partnership has not been created in response to unconscious needs which will emerge within the group and which might lead to conflict (McGee and Schuman, 1970). Prior knowledge and association from other contexts can make for difficulties in forming an adequate contract for the running of the group and maintenance of the co-work relationship. Friendship may be helpful in discovering and working through differences but is no protection against difficulties and no short-cut through preparation for and during the group.

The importance of dialogue is illustrated well by the example of a co-leader joining a groupworker already established within a group. Those in this position can experience difficulty in finding a role and making a contribution in the group and in the co-work relationship. The group's norms will have been set already. The existing groupworker will have established a relationship with the group. If the needs of or dynamics created by the incoming groupworker are not considered, the co-workers may find this experience of groupwork unsatisfying.

The third argument for preparation centres on the fears, expectations and hopes which co-workers will bring to the proposed partnership. These ideas come from a variety of sources not least of which are previous experiences of or fantasies and preconceptions about co-working and group-work. Practitioners may feel hopeful, excited and enthusiastic. They may hope to acquire knowledge or to gain a broader experience of groupwork. They may expect to learn from or to feel at ease with their co-worker, to find creative ways of working which do justice to a combined effort and improve the quality of the group's work. They may expect co-work to be a source of comfort, support and feedback whereby they may gain in confidence as groupworkers or overcome what they feel to be their limited range of skills. They may anticipate that co-working will enable them to learn about themselves and their style of interaction in groups. Equally, they may hope that co-work will enhance the group's work and the workers' ability to work effectively within the group, drawing on the advantages of co-leadership discussed in Chapter Four. In short, the hopes and expectations may be that co-leadership will offer security and protection and enhance satisfaction and pleasure (Dowling, 1979).

However, practitioners may feel apprehensive or nervous. They may be hesitant or ambivalent about co-working or working with a group. These feelings may be inspired by anxieties of not being good enough, by doubts about their personal capabilities and competence. They may view their training as not reflecting the practice skills required in the field or as having alerted them to the problems and complexities without giving them sufficient experience to feel that they can handle them (Parsloe, 1969). They may anticipate that group members will relate more to the co-worker and experience their partner as more capable. Co-leaders may question whether they share an understanding of the group's aims or whether the partnership will fulfil expectations of shared responsibility and mutual support. Common too are doubts about compatibility, whether they share enough common ground or whether different methods of groupwork and differences in experience, working styles and personal characteristics will impede working together. The practitioners may mistrust groups, seeing them as more demanding than casework. They may be concerned about a group's potential for destructiveness or about encountering unmanageable resistance in the group. They may fear losing control of the group or that it will disintegrate because members do not attend or feel that it has anything to offer them. They may fear that hostility will break out in the group, either towards the leaders or other group members, or that members will make overwhelming dependency demands on the leaders. A further fantasy centres on the power of the group to suck the leaders into situations in which they become enmeshed. Groupworkers may hope that co-work will prevent such eventualities. However, groupwork experience does not reduce the presence of these fears initially, even where they have not emerged in previous groups. The fears remain present internally, even for the most experienced groupworkers. Accordingly, if the fears are not to paralyse the leaders and if co-work is to be able to respond creatively to the group, groupworkers need to share their anxieties and images of groups. Otherwise, communication between the practitioners and perceptions of the group are likely to be distorted.

Why prepare for single leadership?

Much the same scenario applies to single leaders. To be a group leader requires the practitioner to be able to tolerate a degree of separateness from the group in order to fulfil their tasks. This position can create its own pressures. The groupworker may respond to these by adopting specific roles to satisfy personal needs and reduce the impact of these pressures. The groupworker may respond by feeling the need to be in control of the group, reflected in a directive, authoritarian approach. Alternatively, they may seek to reduce the expression of emotions in the group. The pressures may lead the groupworker to seek to remain unexposed in the group, reflected either in withdrawal from it or in an over-emphasis on listening and non-directiveness. Again, they may emphasise their expertise in the areas being discussed by the group and their interventions may appear to be intellectual and 'text-book' rather than related to the members' communications. Another type of response to these pressures is seen in the leader wanting to be liked. Here the group-worker emphasises what they share in common with group members or the importance of friendliness, tolerance and positive feelings. Any of these roles can reduce the group's effectiveness in working towards its aims (Williams, 1966).

As with co-leaders, solo practitioners will take into a project hopes, fears, strengths, weaknesses and earlier group experiences. They will need to have the ability to control or contain personal needs and problems if they are to be able to engage the group. They will need to be able to identify their skills and their relevance for the group's tasks. They will need to be flexible in their use of models of groupwork if they are to ensure that the needs and problems of the group are met effectively as they emerge.

The choice of single leadership may result from the absence of a potential or suitable co-leader or from agency practice-wisdom. Alternatively, it may be influenced by the type of group planned or personal preference. This preference may be based either on assumptions about single leadership compared with co-work or on confidence in a personal repertoire of skills. Whatever the route, solo practitioners need to answer some fundamental questions if they are not to react to or interact with a group inappropriately. First, does the modality feel congenial? If it does not, and if the practitioner doubts their ability to run the group, the choice needs to be reconsidered. To answer this question, it may prove helpful to reflect on past experiences of or assumptions about this modality, together with their motives behind the choice. The solo practitioner should consider their confidence and skills in groupwork generally and in relation to this specific task. Secondly, are they interested in this group? The leader needs to anticipate what the group may arouse in them and whether they feel able to participate in the tasks of the group. This involves them considering their fears, feelings and expectations of the group and whether they can make a contribution in the group from the skills and knowledge which they possess.

Techniques

The techniques which follow are described in the belief that they can facilitate positive outcomes by contributing to a focussed discussion on whether the proposed single leadership or co-work relationship is viable for the participants. They offer a means of recognising, using and maximising the strengths of each worker, something which, in my experience, practitioners find difficult. For co-workers, the techniques provide an opportunity to acclimatise themselves to their colleague's working styles. This helps to develop support and mutual understanding and to decide how to cope with difficulties in the group or co-work pairing. They enable the participants to identify and share their knowledge in order to plan responses to group processes and situations. They enable the workers to share and work through their anxieties about working together, such as competitiveness or feelings that the partner will be the more effective group-worker.

Personal profile

This is a useful technique since it requires the individual practitioner to think through their own experiences, knowledge-base, fantasies and expectations. When co-working, these can be shared with the potential colleague to foster the development of mutual trust and understanding. Groupworkers could write out their own profile and structure it as follows:

- what is my social work background?
- what training in social work and groupwork have I received?
- what has been my experience of groups as a member and leader?
- what I have learned from these experiences?
- what is my value-base and preferred style of working?
- what are my interests?
- what is my theoretical orientation (eclectic, psychodynamic, behavioural)?

- where would I place myself on a leadership continuum of active – passive and of directive – non-directive?
- what methods of intervention do I favour?
- what have been my previous experiences of co-working and groupwork?
- what have I learned from these encounters?
- what do I know about groups?
- what do I feel about groups?
- what do I feel able to offer to the co-work relationship and to a group?
- what learning opportunities do I feel able to offer to a colleague?
- what are my expectations of a co-leader and what are my personal learning needs?
- what are my strengths and weaknesses?
- what expectations do I have about being a group leader and about groups?
- what are my hopes and aims which I am bringing to this particular task?

Although a daunting and all-encompassing list, it does enable both the writer of the profile and a co-worker or supervisor to discuss the skills and experiences available to them. It helps them to specify what they are bringing to the task and to identify the presence and relevance of previous experiences, skills and theoretical frameworks. From this base, the participants can assess whether and how they might meet the needs of the group. The profile enables practitioners to pull together their training, experiences of groups, and their fears, fantasies and assumptions about groups. When shared with a co-leader or colleagues, this may enable them to work together positively.

Fantasy Exercise

Here I suggest that practitioners write out and then share their ideal solo practice or co-work relationship. The same may be done with their fantasies of a co-work relationship and of solo practice. These might include the fear that their weaknesses will be exposed in the group. Co-workers may be anxious about whether they can form a good working relationship or about sharing responsibility and control despite wanting to do so.

The rationale for this exercise is that individual practitioners will bring to each new encounter fantasies, expectations and assumptions which are based on previous experiences. If these are not to form the basis of subsequent dissatisfactions and disappointments, they must be acknowledged openly and fully discussed. This may help to diffuse anxieties and ensure that present practice is not impeded unduly by past events.

Sentence completion

The rationale behind this exercise is the belief that it is essential to consider personal characteristics and interpersonal styles. Group members will project fantasies about the workers and their relationship. If these projections are anticipated in advance as well as dealt with in the group, the practitioners should avoid acting them out. The following part-sentences are offered as examples of the types of questions which groupworkers should address:

- what do I need to know about my co-worker to help me understand their thinking?
- I agreed to consider working with this group because . . . (interest; an opportunity to work with this co-worker; or . . .?)
- I want to work alone/with this co-leader because . . .
- my expectations in working alone/with this co-worker are. . .
- my hopes and fears in working alone/with this co-leader are . . .
- things I would prefer my co-leader not to know about me are. . .
- things I think my colleague should know about me are . . . (style, orientation, special interests, theoretical influences, experiences and feelings about co-working).
- the skills which I feel I have as a group leader are . . .

- where conflicts might lie.
- who the groupworkers most wish to please.
- whether differences of opinion concerning the group's aims are due to the workers occupying different positions in the system.
- the obligations and links which co-workers have which might influence how they relate to each other in the group.
- who needs to be consulted.
- any features which make working together problematic.
- where support may be found.

Exercises focussing on the group

At this point of preparation for the group, groupworkers should give some attention not to the specifics of group planning but to what they hope to accomplish with the group, how they might function within it and the roles they might adopt and feel comfortable with. Groupworkers may have an assertive or passive working style. They may prefer either to take on the task-oriented leadership role or the group-maintenance leadership role (Douglas, 1976; Donnellan, 1981). They may see their strength as lying in an ability to keep the group focussed on the task or in bringing specific skills into the group such as techniques like sculpting and psychodrama or skills of observation and interpretation of group dynamics. Potential colleagues need to specify their skills within these role areas and to assess whether they or the partnership has the range of skills which might be required of them in a group.

Co-leadership involves co-operation. It involves taking up and relinquishing leadership, negotiating power and leadership within the relationship. It is helpful, therefore, if practitioners clarify their preferences for leading or responding and their preferred styles of working. In addition, co-workers should assess the effectiveness of their communication and co-operation. Various techniques may prove useful here in illuminating those areas where a more effective balance needs to be achieved, those points where the relationship or an individual practitioner is under strain.

Fantasy House: Holding a pen together and without speaking, co-workers draw their dream house. This may be followed by discussing what happened, how they experienced the exercise, and whether conflict was resolved by domination, submission or reciprocity (Donnellan, 1981).

Describing a shape: Sitting back to back, one co-worker designs a shape and must instruct the partner to draw the shape without using gestures, turning round or telling the partner what the overall shape is. Each partner should have the opportunity to communicate and receive. The workers can discuss then how they experienced the exercise (Donnellan, 1981).

Mirror exercise: One co-worker is nominated as leader and their partner has to mirror everything the leader does. Roles may be reversed and the exercise concluded with neither partner being the nominated leader and with each choosing whether to mirror the actions of the other or to initiate an action of their own (Donnellan, 1981).

Trust games: There are many varieties of trust games but I have found two especially useful. In a trust walk, one partner is blindfolded and let by the co-worker. In a trust fall, one partner falls backwards to be caught by the co-leader.

These exercises will show who prefers leading and initiating, who prefers to respond, and the co-workers' ability to accept and relinquish leadership. It will highlight the co-workers' preferred styles of working and enable them to assess the extent to which they feel comfortable with each other. It will become apparent whether they are able to communicate and trust each other, to be themselves and to express their individuality and differences.

These exercises may be combined with discussion. Particularly important questions here are:

- how comfortable do you feel in taking control of a group or in letting someone else take control?
- what makes you feel uncomfortable in groups?
- how do you respond to tension and conflict in groups?
- how do you respond to disagreements with others?
- how important is it for you to be liked and needed by group members?
- what are your reactions to members whom you find it hard to like?
- how open can you be with group members?
- are your favoured styles of leadership appropriate for the group and, where co-working, are they compatible with those of your partner?
- what would be your attitude and approaches to problems which you anticipate the group might present?
- are your interests and ideas about the group compatible with those of your partner?
- can you, your colleague and supervisor find ways to develop your contributions in the group and to support each other?
- what do you expect of yourself and your partner?
- what are the indicators and necessary conditions for working well together?

This leads into using a formula proposed by Piggin and Watson (1979). They suggest that co-leaders should list those factors which make their particular combination appropriate or inappropriate for the group. Groupworkers should pay special attention then to the inappropriate factors since these could form potential problem areas. Solo practitioners can use this formula also.

The approach I have described will help groupworkers to identify their own needs, expectations and fears and to familiarise themselves with their co-worker's expectations, skills and characteristic approach to problems. I believe that it will contribute to comfortable working and the resolution of unrealistic and distorted expectations and perceptions. Differences in opinion and style can be acknowledged openly and ways found to handle them rather than to minimise them. This approach fosters trust and confidence from which groupworkers can comment critically on each other's performance in the group.

Stages within practice

It would be a misconception to suppose that no further consideration of the co-work relationship or the practice of solo leadership is necessary once some initial preparation has been completed. No co-work relationship can be said to be formed fully at the outset but each is a dynamic entity developing and, hopefully, maturing over time. Equally, no worker can be prepared fully for leadership or their part in the co-work relationship at the beginning of the group. Rather, their experiences can be monitored through several developmental stages (Reynolds, 1965; Heap, 1977; Dick *et al.*, 1980). The stages are not unidirectional and some overlap is inevitable. The later stages may occur only when running a group or after several experiences. The framework below is offered in the hope that it will enable groupworkers to make sense of their experiences. At all points the quality of the work, the comfort of the workers and the speed with which they work through the stages will be influenced by the extent to which, as co-leaders, they have similar orientations, agree on problems existing within their relationship and the group, and are comfortable with the roles each adopts (Paulson *et al.*, 1976). For solo practitioners, progression through the stages and the quality of the work will be influenced by the degree to which they feel comfortable with their roles, are clear about their skills and difficulties, have access to support and clearly conceptualise problems within the group and influences on their practice.

Beginning

In this opening stage, potential groupworkers will be concerned mainly with personal issues. Their feelings may range from enthusiasm and hopeful anticipation to apprehension and nervousness. They may feel that much depends on their skills and be concerned with whether they will be good enough. They may feel that their experience and competence in groupwork is limited and question their ability to deal with issues as they emerge in the group. Individual practitioners will be acutely self-conscious (Reynolds, 1965), experiencing some paralysis, a need to be accepted and not to let themselves down, a need for information and security within a feeling of not knowing. Besides feelings about their identity and performance as groupworkers, the participants will consider their motivation for forming a co-work pairing, the experiences which influence what they bring to the formation, and their coping and defence-mechanisms. There follows an orientation to each other, a concentration on becoming acquainted with and accustomed to each other. It is here that issues of power and control, status, philosophies and communication may emerge, together with early considerations of organising the group from which may come some understanding of the group's aims and of the workers' commitment and compatibility. At this stage the workers are operating more as two individuals than one unit.

Development

Concerns about self-functioning are still influential at this point but inter-personal issues become more prominent. Groupworkers will be gathering information about their own and their co-workers' styles, strengths, and limitations, familiarising themselves with their own or their colleague's skills, capacity to support and confidence. If already leading a group, they will begin to feel able to support each other, utilise each other's strengths and compensate for each other's weaknesses. It is at this phase that some sense of a joint enterprise should develop. The groupworkers will find some agreement as to roles within the partnership and the group and some consensus concerning the group's aims. They will ascertain the degree of similarity about their views and expectations concerning the group, the potential for trust and the ability to pick up each other's cues. They will realise the extent to which there are fears about relinquishing some responsibility and control to the other. It is during this phase that some awareness of the viability of the pairing per se and in respect of the proposed group should emerge. However, both as individuals and as a partnership, interaction and performance will carry a quality of a sink or swim adaptation (Reynolds, 1965), characterised by the beginnings of acquiring and building on knowledge and roles, of seeing what is expected and required but with a continued dependence on approval.

A formed approach, felt to be satisfactory

This is a stage of trust where the workers feel confident and have dealt with their fears and expectations which they brought initially. The atmosphere is one of harmony wherein the participants can seek and value suggestions, learn from others and, when co-working, anticipate each other's actions. Attention can be focussed now much more on preparation for and the actual leadership of the group. Both in respect of the pairing and the group, some re-examination and revision of the group's aims and the roles adopted by the workers may prove necessary (Heap, 1977), perhaps on several occasions until the aims and roles feel clear and congruent with the group's task and the needs, interests and skills of the members and leaders. The workers may experience their activity as being characterised by understanding but without the power to control their performance, by an intellectual grasp but with uncertainty in their ability to translate this into action. There is less self-preoccupation here but the ability to perform tasks may be uneven despite adjustment to new concepts and skills (Reynolds, 1965). Problems may arise if the workers do not feel accepted as individuals with space to express their individuality. This stage, in ideal conditions however, is marked by purposeful activity where the workers are interdependent, drawing on each other.

Full functioning

This is a phase where work appears effortless and is characterised by flexible working, an ability to respond and change according to the needs of and trends within the group. It is marked by a high degree of satisfaction and personal growth and by the use of fresh perspectives and creative innovation. It is within this stage that group members may experience not just techniques but rapid growth and change. Reynolds (1965) has described this phase for practitioners as one of relative mastery. Workers both understand and can control their activity. What was new has become part of the worker's repertoire. Old skills are related to new skills. Self-criticism is possible within an understanding of situations and the demands they make.

Clearly, any groupworker or partnership may revert to earlier stages. Equally, an understanding of each other's ways of working, developed at the outset, will require further development during the group as areas previously not considered arise. Finally, as the workers move through these phases, the group itself and the interaction of the workers with the group become more prominent.

Conclusion

This chapter has outlined how groupworkers may prepare themselves for groupwork either as single practitioners or co-workers. Preparation influences outcome and solo or co-work without it is inadvisable, especially since the effectiveness of a group is related to the dynamics, qualities and vicissitudes of the individual workers or co-work relationship (McGee and Schuman, 1970). It may not be possible to guarantee that workers will work well together even after preparation, nor indeed to cover every eventuality, but it is an essential beginning.

6

Working with a Group

Introduction

When a group works well, it can be highly productive. When it does not, it can prove frustrating. This chapter will concentrate on how practitioners can increase their effectiveness and that of the group, on how they can promote the development of the group's cohesion and work.

Of fundamental importance to the operation of the group is how groupworkers work within it and co-leaders work together. However thorough the preparation and initial interviews, the group will need skilled help to move from a collection of individuals towards developing a common purpose and sense of cohesion where members feel valued for their contribution and able to engage in the group's tasks. Groupworkers may be preoccupied still with doubts about their capacity to retain members or to cope with events in groups such as silence or the expression of hostility, anger and criticism. The actual group experience may uncover problems between co-workers not apparent in preparation or indicate the need to revise the roles and activities which had been planned.

During the group the workers will change and develop. At the outset they may feel inadequate, under-used or de-skilled, with little to offer. Gradually, confidence may increase and co-workers may develop a productive balance between separateness and togetherness, individuality and integration. Therefore, groupworkers should be prepared to acknowledge and explore these changes, work at integrating their emerging skills and adapt their functioning in the group in response to their personal development. In short, the co-work relationship and the leaders' inter-relationship with the group needs to be worked on continuously, evaluated and modified in response to dynamics within the group and the leaders.

The first meeting

Right beginnings are vital. How the group begins will influence members' attitudes to the group, each other, the leaders and the group's objectives. Joining a group is not easy. Members may find the idea of a group strange despite having discussed its formation, general aims and the possible benefits with the groupworkers. They may be puzzled or suspicious about its purpose and the groupworkers' roles. They may experience heightened anxiety from uncertainty about what to expect, how they will be perceived or whether the group will help them. They may anticipate that the demands made of them will be strange and possibly threatening. They may fear rejection, either exaggerating their difficulties to demonstrate their need for help or minimising these to gain respect. They may believe groups to be inferior to individual sessions with social workers. They may view the workers' authority differently from the leaders themselves or regard the group as punitive or compulsory when the leaders view it as therapeutic and supportive. Whether or not membership is compulsory and the group formed or pre-dating the social workers' involvement with it, members may come with a positive attitude towards it or with ambivalence, defensiveness and aggression. If these feelings remain unacknowledged they can impede members engaging in the group experience, prove traumatic and disturbing, or foster insecurity and anger.

From the initial interviews, leaders and members will enter the group with some information regarding the group's structure, purpose and aims and individual members' needs, problems or goals. However, groupworkers should not assume that the goals or the nature of their participation are clear. Each member will have a relationship with the leaders from having discussed their feelings about the group and listened to information provided by the leaders. In natural groups members will have established some norms and links between themselves. The task is to develop a common perception of and investment in the tasks and to clarify the groupworkers' roles and purposes. To assume a consensus or to hurry progress towards it is to risk an ineffective group. Consensus will develop only after a detailed expression of expectations, concerns, reservations, aims and procedures. If there is a gap between the leaders' and members' aims and expectations, to ignore this will interfere with the group's process and outcome. Therefore, it is important not just to work on the assumed tasks but to reconsider the group's aims and how it is to function. Contracts made with individuals should be re-examined and, if necessary, renegotiated. Despite having negotiated a contract prior to the group, members may express their needs differently in the first sessions. To assume that they know why they are there and want to be fails to recognise that they may not feel they have a choice. Renegotiation may result in some members feeling that they should withdraw at this stage.

If the group is to make a difference for members and if they are to participate actively, groupworkers must communicate the opportunities presented by the group. It is not easy to communicate the group's purpose and possible gains in advance of actually experiencing the group. However, this task of raising motivation and confidence in members who may be uncertain is helped by groupworkers making their intentions specific, being clear about why they are there and not defining aims so broadly that they are limitless, for instance to increase self-confidence.

A structure for the first meeting might run as follows: First, general introductions, perhaps using name games (Brandes and Phillips, 1978). Secondly, groupworkers provide some information about themselves to the group, especially concerning their interest in this group, their previous experience and their agency's hopes for the group. Members should be invited to ask questions.

Thirdly, discuss with members how control is to be

exercised and problems tackled in the group. Setting norms at the outset makes it easier for the group to take responsibility for its functioning. Accordingly (Hodge, 1985):

- what are the group's behavioural norms? How are members expected to behave and relate in the group?
- what rules and sanctions are to be set? Does the agency set any limits?
- what is the group's attitude to late arrivals, regularity of attendance and rule-bending?
- what action will be taken if members miss sessions or attend infrequently? Will the leaders or some members visit the non-attenders?
- what is confidential to the group? What will be or needs to be shared outside the group?
- what power do the members have to make rules?
- how will the leaders or members exercise control in the group? The waiting game (Brandes and Phillips, 1978) is a useful technique for bringing some order to a group.

Fourthly, it may be appropriate for the groupworkers to discuss their authority with the group, not in a general sense but specifically in relation to the group. Authority may be expressed in several ways. There may be situations in which the leaders would want to stress their positional authority to authorise or prohibit behaviour, this authority arising from their position in their agency or from their position as group leaders. They may choose to stress their sapiential authority, that is authority invested in them by members because they are seen as knowledgeable or appropriate models. Or they may choose to stress the members' authority. However, members may view the leaders' authority differently from the workers themselves. For example, the leaders may wish to be seen as models or to be as uninfluential as possible but the members may see them as representatives of an agency which has ultimate power over them or as figures who possess information and expertise or the power to authorise or prohibit behaviour. These perceptions will affect how members see the leaders and interact in the group. If differences in perceptions remain unacknowledged, aims for the group may remain divergent.

Fifthly, discuss the group's purpose and structure. Members are more likely to remain in the group if the group begins from where they are, if they feel that they can obtain satisfaction from membership, and if their apprehensions are acknowledged openly. This, and the development of cohesion and consensus, is helped where the group's task is clear, where the aims and purposes are negotiated and where specific objectives are formulated within the overall aims. Useful pointers here include:

- what are the members' expectations? What do they want? Why are they present? Distinguish between motivation and persuasion to attend since the latter can be demotivating.
- what might they be asked to do?
- what are individuals' needs, problems and contract? How do they explain their problems or circumstances? What is needed in the group?
- explain why members were chosen. Establish the group's boundaries: can friends attend and will new members be admitted?
- what can the leaders offer the group (for example, information on the structure of welfare services, experience in developing a strategy or finding an effective method of organising the group, knowledge of local resources)?
- why are the leaders and agency interested in this group?
- anticipate possible reactions, attitudes, resistances and areas of commonality. Connect the members. Acknowledge feelings and encourage their expression, especially relating to membership. Are there any stumbling blocks to engagement?
- locate and discuss any problems between members and between them and the leaders.
- what content? How might the goals be achieved (discussion, activity, campaigns)?
- how negotiable is the programme with members? Who sets the agenda? Will the leaders suggest their ideas? The advantages of members deciding the agenda is that the group begins where the members are and it encourages them to contribute their own resources. The drawbacks

are that it can mean a slower beginning to sessions and raise members' anxiety. One way forward here is to plan each session jointly.

The more realistic and relevant the aims, the better group-workers will be able to:

- give members a clear basis for accepting the offer of a group and for making alternative or supplementary suggestions concerning aims or activities.
- assist the group in finding a relevant content and style.
- evaluate whether or not the aims are being achieved and whether the group has reached the point of termination.
- recognise where they need to intervene.

Finally, write out a group contract to cover the following points:

- agreed goals, the issues being dealt with and the identified targets for change.
- group rules.
- what is expected of members, particularly in terms of attendance and participation.
- what the leaders are offering and what they will assume responsibility for.

Any contract should be renegotiable to take account of developments in the group and to give members some means of controlling their involvement with it. Equally important, a contract can be formalised only if the groupworkers can commit themselves to it given their setting and agency responsibilities.

This structure may take more than one session to complete and it should not be rushed because this approach does seem to enhance members' commitment and to facilitate the group's process and outcomes. The groupworkers' task is to promote the group's existence as a group, an objective which may require that they summarise what needs to be dealt with, acknowledge different views, involve quiet members and point out areas of commonality.

Work within sessions

The groupworkers' manner of interaction within the group is crucial. A careful balance is needed between the achievement of tasks and the pace of the work since, if members feel that the costs of membership exceed the rewards, they may not attend and, once the group has begun to work, their initial motivation may diminish for a time if they sense that change or the group's work may be difficult. Groupworkers can help the group to work by:

- beginning each meeting with a group round: reviewing the last session and the week's events; evaluating progress within and outside the group.
- taking up feelings about the group and acknowledging difficulties presented by the group's tasks.
- discussing whether the group is what members expected or whether they feel that it is meeting their needs.
- reframing the group's initial material into specific objectives or connecting subsequent themes to these objectives. This will assist the group in devising a programme and in identifying indicators by which to assess progress towards achieving the set objectives.
- checking whether the actions of the leaders carried different meanings for members than those intended by the groupworkers.
- creating a warm, comfortable atmosphere where members feel that they are accepted and belong.
- providing opportunities for members to help each other and identifying their resources, for example for collective action, support and acceptance, and control or confrontation of each other's problems or self-image.
- promoting interaction in the group, involving members with each other.
- stressing that the problems or circumstances of individual members are not unique. Providing opportunities for members to acquire knowledge, to see how others tackle similar difficulties and to examine their own solutions and test out new behaviours.
- enabling members to voice their concerns and express their feelings.

– ensuring that the programme for each session is clear and
  sufficient for the time available.

Disagreement between co-workers is healthy and useful
but competitiveness and hostility is not. Once the group is
established, co-leaders should discuss any concerns about
the group within it and resolve any difficulties or different
ideas by discussing the issues and possible options and
deciding on a course of action. This modelling of dialogue
may help to reduce members' defensiveness and contributes
to the group's vitality and growth and to the leaders' functioning. How members experience the co-work relationship and
whether its effectiveness and potential is realised or not will
depend on how the leaders respond to differences between
them, on how far they are able to share their thoughts and
develop support and complementarity. If they can find a
means of expressing differences without seeming to be
undermining or invalidating the other, members may find
confidence to express their views and feel that the expression
of differences is not necessarily destructive (Hodge, 1985).

Work outside the sessions

Whatever prior decisions groupworkers have made concerning their roles within the group, the events within it,
how they experience them and how members perceive the
groupworkers may necessitate some revision. Change does
not reflect an inability to be consistent but may be an
appropriate response to the members' emerging needs. If
leadership is to meet the group's needs appropriately, regular consultation and reviews of the groupworkers' roles and
developing practice skills and of the group's dynamics and
goals are important components in effective work.

Specifically, planning prior to each session should focus
on:

– ensuring that they have a frame of reference for the
  meeting. Are the plan, sharing of tasks, aims and responsibilities clear?
– reviewing their goals and strategies, ensuring that they

share an understanding of their roles in the group. Each new phase of work needs to be planned. They need to decide how to handle problems within the group or their partnership. They need to identify their likes, dislikes and feelings towards the members and the issues or problems they bring to the group, especially where these have some similarities with the leaders' own life situations or difficulties.

- considering any unresolved matters between the co-leaders. Unresolved or latent conflicts between them may be stirred up by the experience of leading a group. They should avoid private conceptualisations of events in the group since if these and inevitable points of difference or conflict remain unexpressed, they may create negative consequences within the group. Therefore, it is helpful for co-workers to discuss how they affect and perceive each other: their satisfactions, dissatisfactions and difficulties in working together.
- acknowledging their own 'baggage' which is unrelated to the group, such as the influence of their personal lives on their functioning as groupworkers. Co-workers can compensate for a leader who feels tired or without motivation.
- sharing their thoughts and views about the group.

There is a clear relationship between a group's effectiveness and the time and thought given to preparation, planning and discussion. Meetings after each group meeting are a means of avoiding discrepancies in how the leaders perceive the group's tasks and development, of releasing tension taken out of the group and of ensuring that roles and objectives are understood and clear. An agenda for these meetings should include:

- recording.
- reviewing previous sessions: what progress is being made? What works within the group? Are there any alliances within the group and do these interfere with or promote the group's task and members' development? How are the group's resources developing? What is emerging in the group or preoccupying members? Are there particular problems or processes within the group which need to

be tackled? Are adjustments necessary to objectives, methods or activities? Are the groupworkers' skills, styles and theoretical orientations helpful to the group? Sensitivity to changing needs and group development is an important skill and adjusting to these needs or developments is a critical factor in effectiveness.
- planning future sessions: what preparation is necessary? What are the goals and what next steps are appropriate? How can the group consolidate what has been achieved? What tasks will each leader undertake?
- analyse the interaction between the groupworkers and between them and the group.

Taking the interaction between the groupworkers, some reflection is required on their feelings about the sessions involving feedback and criticism. Useful questions here are:

- how well do they feel they worked together and supported each other?
- what did they like and dislike about the other in the sessions?
- in what areas do they feel improvements in their working relationship are needed and how might these be achieved?
- how have their hopes and fears about the partnership worked out in the group?
- do they feel able within the partnership to develop their own style and skills?
- in what ways is this experience developing their knowledge and skills? What are they learning?
- are there discrepancies between what groupworkers think they are doing and what their colleagues think they are doing?
- are roles clearly differentiated? Are the roles they adopted initially still appropriate? How are the roles they are adopting in the group working out? What roles are they taking in the group?

Concerning the interaction between groupworkers and members, useful questions here include:

- what was their effect on the group and the group's effect on them?

- are members attempting to split the leaders? Is this inter-fering with the work? Effectiveness is promoted where splitting is confronted openly in meetings. Does it indicate that members feel ambivalent or resentful about member-ship or are members relating to an imbalance in the groupworkers' experience and expertise? Does it reflect one colleague deferring to the other or is it related to the roles and styles they are using in the group?
- are co-workers mirroring the group's behaviour, repro-ducing in their relationship patterns observed in the group? For example, are the co-workers competitive, wanting to be the best liked, most insightful? Are they adopting roles of expert or authority figure, or over-emphasising listening, intellectualisation, withdrawal and over-identification with members as a defence, a security operation in response to material in the group or to doubts about their groupwork skills? Are the co-workers feeling depressed, angry or guilty, feelings which have been transferred from members and which can be mistaken as their own feelings (Hodge, 1985)? Is the group making them feel inadequate or not in control of the group or themselves? This evaluation will help the groupworkers to make sense of what they are experiencing and to plan their future interactions with and interventions in the group.

Common problems

Many things happen in groups. The purpose of this section is to examine some of these, the prospect of which, in my experience, concern groupworkers.

Scapegoating

A scapegoat is a member who is isolated, attacked or ac-corded low status and onto whom the group projects feelings it finds unacceptable or views it holds. Until these are addressed the group will maintain this situation, the process diverting energy from the group's tasks. The scapegoat will

but there are reasons which lead them to avoid attempting to solve the problem (Douglas, 1976). Once again, it is necessary to review the group's tasks and take up the dynamics which are interfering with working towards the accomplishment of the tasks.

Dominant members

Sometimes one or several members dominate the group and compete with one another or the leaders. This domination can result in other members contributing little to decision making or to the group's process. Equally, it can divert the focus away from the work of the group.

It is important for groupworkers to understand and raise within the group the meaning behind this domination. For example, it may represent a fear of close relationships or of not being heard, or it may be members' habitual ways in which they behave in groups and attempt to elicit attention or care-giving. In my opinion, besides attempting to bring in other members into the discussion or group's activities and interpreting directly to the dominant member the meanings underlying their interaction with the group, the use of circular questioning can be effective in dealing with this group dynamic. Useful questions here might include:

- what does the dominant member think other members might say? Do they agree?
- how does the dominant member think other members' view their contribution in the group? Do they agree or disagree and in what respects?
- who in the group most/least agrees with this member?

The clown

A member may adopt this role either as a defence against anxiety or close relationships or to conceal the absence of social ease. Once again, the meaning of this behaviour must be understood and, through using other members, explored if the individual is to be enabled to test out other ways of behaving and relating.

Sub-groups

The development of sub-groups may indicate apprehension about meaningful involvement in the group or disagreement with the task. They may indicate that the group has yet to find an effective means of working as a group. Alternatively, sub-groups can promote the group's cohesiveness by involving isolated or quiet members who may find it difficult to contribute in the whole group. As such they can be a means of putting members in touch with each other. However, where sub-groups have rigid boundaries and exclude other members, they are unlikely to promote the group's effectiveness. If the groupworkers have not deliberately formed sub-groups as part of the group's work, they need to understand and interpret the meaning behind their formation and discuss with members their effect on the group.

Dependency on the leaders

In some groups, for example with children, leaders may retain responsibility for creating and maintaining the group's framework, aims and boundaries. However, although dependent to some extent on the type of group, the leaders' overall aim should be to hand back gradually to the group responsibility for its functioning. One rationale for this is that many members will have the resources to direct the group and that, if the leaders remain central to the group, they may de-skill these members. Another rationale is that, if members can develop these skills within the group, there is an increased likelihood that the gains they make in the group will be sustained outside it when the group has terminated and the support of the groupworkers is no longer available. However, it is a difficult task. It requires the leaders to keep pace with members' skills and development. Further, members may perceive the groupworkers as holding the leadership function and a position of experts, in addition to which they may be used to occupying a subordinate, passive position. The leaders may be expected to have ideas about how the group should develop and to be directive when the groupworkers are seeking to emphasise members' resources and responsibilities for the group's direction and development.

If indeed the groupworkers are aiming to become less central to the group, they should make this explicit at the outset and outline what they believe to be the members' responsibilities and what they will contribute to the group. Further, throughout the group, they should review their roles with the members and point out the group's increasing resources to use and direct the group purposefully.

Conflict between members or with the leaders

Conflict can be demonstrated in a number of ways. Members may express frustration with or hostility towards one another. They may ridicule or disagree with each other's suggestions. They may dispute the leaders' suggestions and argue that the group will not be effective. There are three reasons for this conflict (Douglas, 1976). The group may feel that its task is impossible and members may feel unable to meet the demands made of them. The conflict may be symbolic of a search for status in the group. Members may feel loyal to outside systems, such as peers or family members, whose interests or demands conflict with the group's aims. However, conflict is not necessarily negative. It may highlight members' involvement in the group's task and willingness to suggest directions for its efforts. It may represent impatience or disagreement with current approaches to and solutions for the group's goals.

Groupworkers may feel it necessary to control the conflict where it threatens to disrupt the group, perhaps through using the waiting game. Otherwise, disagreements should be summarised and the meaning behind them explored in order that members can agree on the tasks and how they are to be approached.

Stages in a group

Groups develop and change, passing through stages which can be conceptualised (Tuckman, 1965; Heap, 1977). The duration of any stage is related more to the group's history, context and dynamics, and to the groupworkers' skills than to time, although in short-term groups the latter stages may not be reached. The stages are not sequential or unidirectional necessarily, nor will every group experience every stage because of time limitations or difficulties within it. A group may be at different stages for different tasks. The value of conceptualising groups in this way lies in enabling groupworkers to tune into the group's process and respond appropriately.

Stage One: Joining

This stage, sometimes called forming (Tuckman, 1965), is characterised by separateness, difficulty in sharing and an absence of cohesion. Members may have accepted the groupworkers' explanations that they share similar problems and experiences. However, they may have reservations about the group's viability and membership, particularly when they know very little about the others and why they are there. Members will be anxious: are people like me? How do they react to me? Should I invest myself in this group? When do I speak? How much do I disclose and discuss? This stage is marked by members seeking similarities, shared interests and background, values and attitudes from which to develop commonality, norms and a definition of themselves in relation to the group's tasks and their role within these. A hierarchy and leader, often the most assertive member, may emerge. Members may seem dependent on the groupworkers, especially for approval and guidance, but this may be accompanied by suspicion of the leaders' intentions, anxiety about the group's tasks or testing out the leaders' understanding, reliability, authority and concern.

Groupworkers are central in this stage by virtue of their

positional authority and having brought the group together or offered their services to an already formed group. They should aim to demonstrate that members have something to offer each other, that their resources are information for the group. They should decide the style of introductions and guide the group in establishing communication and defining roles consistent with the group's goals. Their task is to emphasise the aims, functions and boundaries of the group, to hold the structure open and to prevent domination by individual members. Their task is to open up issues rather than offer definitive answers, to instil confidence, to anticipate members' concerns about the group and to focus on members' hopes rather than perceived deficiencies. Concerning the group's emotional and maintenance needs, leaders should facilitate the search for commonality, helping members express and compare expectations and locate common problems. This, together with attending to individual needs, may promote interaction. Too passive an approach may undermine cohesion. Too authoritarian an approach may result in over-reliance on the leaders' and underestimation of the group's resources. This approach may push the group too far too fast or fail to begin where the members are.

Stage Two: Beginning the work

This stage is marked by growing cohesion and interpersonal ties. Members will attempt to perform as a group, identify with it and develop clarity and consensus about its objectives. The group works towards an agenda of issues, begins to analyse why the problems or issues on the agenda exist and establishes what action to take (Mullender and Ward, 1985). Members will begin to share and explore relationships within the group: who members are and why they are there. Initial roles may becomes established, for example who leads and who withdraws, as members work out the kind of organisation or structure most appropriate to the group's tasks. There may be some dispute and testing out of roles, for instance over leadership of the group, but the emphasis is more on conformity than challenge in order to keep the experience 'good' and avoid confrontation. Members will begin to develop a sense of what is required but may depend still on approval and may be uncertain about their performance in the group. In this stage, sometimes referred to as storming and norming (Tuckman, 1965), members may question the usefulness and aims of the group but identify with and commit themselves to it, establishing rules and norms. They may react with optimism on finding that other members share their concerns but also with anxiety and hopelessness when they realise that there is more to membership than just sharing these issues. This stage is a process of finding a way to make a contribution to the group and of coping with the problems of being a member. Once a purpose and structure have been identified, members work out a code of practice and behaviour. Individuals come with attitudes, opinions, beliefs and values. These are modified and extended in early group sessions, from which members agree on standards of behaviour and rules in order to accomplish tasks and maintain cohesiveness.

The leaders' role concerning the group's task needs is to help members use the group. This may involve opening up issues, involving all the members, and clarifying what the leaders will and will not do. It involves transferring responsibility to members for the group gradually, offering feedback and comments rather than controlling direction. It may involve checking their perceptions of the group with members or attempting to introduce flexibility into the group's structure. Concerning the group's emotional needs, the workers' tasks may include attempts to maximise unity and security, to demonstrate understanding and their availability as a resource, or to offer support and guidance. If members do express hopelessness, this may be because they doubt that the group will have an impact or have yet to find a means of approaching their tasks. By identifying resources within and outside the group and by providing guidance on how the group might approach its tasks, the groupworkers may enable the group to progress. Again, too little or too much control and the group will not become cohesive and effective since both approaches reduce the learning opportunities available to members.

Stage Three: Revision

The group may return to this stage several times or, if the original definition of aims proves sufficient, this stage may not be necessary. This phase is characterised by a questioning of original aims or of the group's norms, structure, duration and behaviour as they have evolved. It is an opportunity to identify areas of competence within the group, to clarify its purposes and to modify its aims and norms. The group may review what has been achieved and reanalyse both why the problems or issues on the agenda exist and the actions they decided to take. The group may reaffirm the original issues to be addressed and the actions decided at the outset or may identify new issues or different actions. Clearly, the shorter the group, the less likely this process is to occur.

The workers' role is to ensure a clear articulation of the new aims and to endeavour to be less central in the group. Through this process members may experience gaining some control over their lives and decisions and how others perceive them (Mullender and Ward, 1985).

Stage Four: Renewed emphasis on the work

This phase, which may occur several times following revision, is performing (Tuckman, 1965). It is marked by clearer and purposive aims where the group's influence on members is high, cohesion is strong and the structure stable. Members co-operate in the group's tasks, whether specific problem-solving or decision-making activities. Interaction is marked by increasing experimentation, room to change and an ability to be different. Leadership is diffused throughout the group.

In this phase, the workers should stress the members' authority which comes from their life experience, skills, knowledge and strengths. Other tasks include maximising members' self-esteem, defining the emerging structure and reminding the group of the objectives if members are concentrating on the potency and uniqueness of the group. Finally, leaders should pull back from major responsibility for the group and emphasise members' abilities to provide support, direction and control.

Stage Five: A well-functioning group

This phase is marked by a high level of functioning and movement towards objectives. There is a well-developed and accepted structure where there are specialised and interdependent roles, well established patterns of problem-solving and decision-making, stable relationships and strong interpersonal ties. The group is characterised by flexible working with effective procedures for achieving and adapting to change. The workers are not central to the running of the group.Their task is to promote individual capabilities (Heap, 1977).

Stage Six: Termination

Once a group develops its own life and identity, it can be very difficult to bring it to an end. Tuckman (1965) refers to this as the mourning stage and there are some typical responses to the ending phase (Garland *et al.*, 1968):

1. Denial: members 'forget' that the leaders told them of time-limits and show surprise.
2. Regression: members revert to a less independent level of functioning. Old conflicts and earlier feelings re-emerge. Members show anger to each other or to the groupworkers. Anxiety may increase.
3. Expression of need: members may hope that the leaders will continue to run the group if they show that they still need help. They may present new problems or ones that they have learned will retain the leaders' interest.
4. Recapitulation: detailed recall of earlier experiences in the group's life.

5. Evaluation: detailed discussions of the value of the group experience, its meaning and its worth. Achievements are identified.
6. Flight: this may appear either as a destructive reaction, denying the positive meaning of the group experience, in which members behave in a rejecting or rejection-provoking way, or as a positive reaction in which constructive moves are made towards disengagement and separation, towards developing other interests and relationships, and increased individuality.
7. Other possibilities include the expression of sadness, anger, closeness, satisfaction and proposals for the group to continue.

Each of these reactions may be used as a device to avoid facing up to the pain of termination. Some of them can be used also to face up to and cope with the ending.

Social workers tend to endure considerable guilt about the damage they may inflict by ending experiences which vulnerable people have enjoyed in contrast to many other relationships. Groupworkers may struggle with closure, experiencing difficulty in reflecting on the positive advantages of helping members experience and cope with endings as non-rejecting. The following suggestions are offered as possible means of facilitating an experience of ending which is non-rejecting:

1. Be clear about the projected ending date. Do not start groups for which there is no planned closure date. Relate the group's length to its aims and build in revision since initial decisions are only 'guesstimates'.
2. Share plans about endings with potential referrers and members.
3. Keep the planned time-limit in view throughout the group's life, for example by counting down the sessions and questioning whether it is appropriate to conclude as planned or to continue in some form.
4. Begin to talk more specifically about the end of the group. What will members miss and what will they take away from the group? What do they feel about the group and how might they replace it? What will stay with them

in terms of friendships, gains, losses, achievements, learning or insights? This should be done well before the group's close. It may be painful for members who may find it difficult to understand why the group is ending and why they cannot be offered another.

5. Devote some time to specific discussion and evaluation of what the group has achieved, what progress has been made with individual and group contracts, and try to help members take away some account of personal and collective achievements.

6. Small gifts, photographs, booklets or a special activity can be used as symbols of non-rejecting endings.

7. A follow-up or reunion can be used in the same way and also to reinforce the group's work. Follow-up can be used to identify whether gains made in the group have been sustained or whether some further work is indicated.

Whichever of these approaches to ending are used, the groupworkers' central task is to help members recognise and acknowledge their feelings of sadness and loss, though these may be mixed with feelings of increased autonomy and pride in achievements. Groupworkers also need to be prepared for the expression, sometimes directly but more often indirectly, of negative, rejecting or rejection-provoking behaviour. This should not be ignored or denied but equally leaders need to beware of being trapped by guilt into premature or inappropriate offers of further help. Therefore, the idea of revision is critically important. The group may require more time to achieve its aims or progress may prove to be either more gradual or quicker than expected. Where there has been some progress, the group should continue if there appears to be the potential for further change and if clear aims can be formulated or if consolidation of the work already achieved cannot take place without the groupworkers' intervention. Put another way, it is desirable if ending is related to progress made, if only to prevent members becoming part of a revolving door syndrome.

Equally important when thinking about termination is a focus on the ending of the co-work relationship. Some of the suggestions offered above in relation to the group may be

useful for social workers as they acknowledge the termination of their partnership, their feelings of loss (for example,
of an interesting piece of work), and evaluate the relationship in terms of the skills they have learned through the
experience. The supervisor has a role here in helping groupworkers tease out what they have learned about groupwork
and co-work, what they will take away with them and
whether their views about ending reflect fears of dependency
from members. Supervision may provide the forum in which
they can incorporate knowledge and confidence gained from
this experience explicitly into their practice, setting fresh
objectives and personal goals.

Conclusion

This chapter has described a structure which can increase the
groupworkers' confidence and effectiveness and enable the
group to work productively. In working with a group, it is
helpful to distinguish between the group's tasks, maintenance needs and process. A group engages in its tasks,
aiming to achieve its goals through work and activities.
Varied activities are helpful in overcoming restlessness and
in providing a stimulating, enjoyable experience. Themes
will emerge, disappear and reappear. These themes may
represent anxieties shared by members, a group feeling or
problems for or within the group. It is helpful to acknowledge these themes and enable the group to explore them
through using open-ended comments which invite interaction rather than definitive statements which invite closure.

In relation to a group's maintenance needs, the major task
is to strengthen the group's structure. This may require that
the groupworkers involve the quieter members or summarise and promote communication and problem-solving in the
group. It may involve pointing to resources in the group or
informing members of external resources available to them.
The process is the way the group undertakes its activities.
When the group becomes stuck, the first priority is to understand the meaning of this stuckness. The group's aims or
methods of achieving them may not be clear or dynamics

within the group may be preventing members from engaging in the tasks. Groupworkers may free the group by pointing out interactions within it such as rivalry and focussing the group on enabling members to work through personal feelings and problems that have arisen as a result of group processes. Alternatively, groupworkers may need to offer the group guidance on how to approach the tasks it has set.

Working with a group provides groupworkers with learning opportunities but can also be stressful when they experience the power of group dynamics, encounter difficulties which cloud the way forward, or doubt the effectiveness of their work. The final two chapters of this book, in discussing supervision and evaluation, aim to provide structures which, in addition to those outlined above, can enable groupworkers to work through difficulties and extend the boundaries of what groupwork can achieve for members and groupworkers alike.

7

Supervision

Introduction

The philosophy behind this chapter is that supervision is essential for effective co-working and groupwork. Indeed, neither are appropriate without it. First of all the rationale for supervision of the co-work relationship and of the workers' preparation for and leadership of the group will be outlined. Then the factors which need to be considered when choosing a supervisor will be highlighted. Finally, there will be an outline of what should form the focus for supervision at the various stages of the co-work relationship and work with the group.

Why supervision?

Many groupworkers undertake co-work and groupwork without supervision. They may doubt its relevance or feel that time constraints prohibit it. The agency may not require groupworkers to arrange supervision nor may any employees feel able to take on this task. I believe that such views are a mis-judgement. Even for experienced groupworkers there is value in having a supervisor. The argument to support this view falls into six sections.

1. *The demands of co-work*: Co-leadership is a complex relationship of central importance in the group. Like any relationship difficulties may arise which, if not resolved, may

prove counter-productive. The participants may become competitive, undermine each other in the search for acceptance by the group, or collude with each other against or with the group. The distribution of tasks may be uneven or roles may become rigid rather than changing in line with developments in the group or in the leaders' confidence and skills. Finally, the co-work relationship is in itself a group within the group, with its own dynamic process. If co-work issues remain unresolved the progress of the group may be inhibited and the co-workers unable to carry out their intended tasks (Levine and Dang,1979). Therefore, when forming a partnership and throughout the group the participants should check impressions and concerns, their ability to communicate clearly, and whether any differences or difficulties exist. Supervision can assist the workers in understanding and developing their relationship and resolving areas of difficulty.

2. *The demands of solo leadership*: A practitioner may choose this modality for further training and experience or because they are confident in the task and their ability. They may have failed to identify a suitable co-worker, their interest in or a pressing need for the group providing the impetus for continuing. Alternatively, the choice might have originated in clear and appropriate reasons to 'go it alone'. It may stem from a personal preference for greater autonomy or be based on assumptions that it facilitates role clarity, is more economical in terms of time, or is less threatening to members.

Supervision may help the practitioner to identify the reasons for this modality choice and to explore the appropriateness of this method for the practitioner and the group. A supervisor can help the worker to explore any assumptions about this method. It does not follow that decision making is any easier or aims simpler to define because of the absence of a co-leader. Indeed, this modality is an onerous responsibility. It places greater pressure on the workers by virtue of their being limited to their own skills and resources in understanding and using the group's dynamics and process and in coping with the stress of groupwork. The practitioner may feel isolated and vulnerable, aware of having a lot to take in and manage and of the consequent danger of missing important developments or losing clarity by becoming enmeshed in the group. Leaving aside the question of whether these views actually emerge in practice, supervision may help to offset these anxieties and the limitations of this approach. A supervisor can help leaders explore their involvement in the group, retain clear aims and maintain enthusiasm and direction.

3. *The demands of groupwork*: Initially at least, groupworkers may experience considerable anxiety and defensive reactions may be prominent. Groupworkers may harbour fears and fantasies about working with groups. Together with concerns about how they might be evaluated by group members or co-workers, these feelings may result in the workers adopting various roles as defences. Supervision provides a forum in which workers can identify their fears and anxieties and explore how they might maximise the potential of the group and of themselves or the co-work partnership. If the practitioners feel enmeshed, over-involved or overwhelmed in the group, the more detached view of the supervisor might help the groupworkers to clarify what is happening in the group and how they might intervene effectively.

4. *Issues in groupwork*: Supervision is a useful forum for discussing anticipated or actual difficulties in groupwork and for confronting practice-related questions which occur in the setting-up of a group. Practice-related questions and concerns are probably easy to identify. Accordingly supervision may be concerned with how the workers might handle termination of the group and deal with their feelings, and those of the group members, that the group's work remains unfinished. Supervision may be concerned with encouraging the workers to reflect on their experience of the group and what they have learned. When planning the group, the supervisor may assist the practitioners in deciding the length and membership of the group and in delineating their authority. During the group the leaders may welcome support

in coping with the members' expression of powerful emotions and in finding ways to involve them in commenting on the effectiveness of the group. Throughout, the supervisor can be a source of support and confirmation, someone who enables the workers to clarify their roles and goals and the extent to which their actions are promoting the group's aims.

No less important, but probably more difficult to identify and discuss in supervision, are questions concerning the practitioners' values, attitudes and philosophy concerning groupwork. These will underpin and influence the goals they hope that the group will achieve and their subsequent analysis of the group's content. Supervision may help to clarify whether the group should be concerned with work with individuals in a group format, focussing on individual members' problems, or with systems within which group members exist. In other words, a supervisor can assist practitioners formulate whether their goals and those of members are individual-centred or aiming for social change and whether the leaders will be defining the issues for the group or encouraging members to do so. Linked with this focus is the desirability of defining the resources in the group and the extent to which the group's potential for support, mutual control or collective power can help shape the group's goals or be used in attaining them.

Taking one issue as an example, a common fear at the beginning of a group is whether members will come and whether they will feel that the group has something to offer them. In response to this practitioners may find it difficult to allow members time to form gradually into a cohesive group and to not over-plan the group. Supervision is a forum where workers may take their feelings which have been stimulated by the work. It provides an opportunity for sharing and managing personal issues which may affect the work. It offers a second opinion of encouragement and support for risk-taking and innovation. It is a professional forum for formulating strategy and maintaining a consistent approach over time.

5. *Monitoring of the work*: In conjunction with the group-workers, the supervisor monitors the progress of the group

towards the stated aims and checks that the work is carried out. The supervisor has a role in ensuring standards of service and needs to be aware of what occurs in the group in order to help the practitioners assess whether the power of the group is rendering them ineffective or exposing the group or some of its members to possible harm. The supervisor is involved too in ensuring that the aims and standards of the agency are being realised and in decisions relating to which groups are organised. The supervisor may be the link between the group and its leaders and the agency within which the group is functioning. This role includes not just a responsibility to ensure consistency with agency practice, policy and function, and that the leaders remain in touch with these, but also supporting the leaders in their attempts to change an agency's approach and attitudes to a particular client group.

At both the stage of deciding whether to co-work and during the life of the group, a supervisor may comment on the progress of the co-work relationship and of the group, locate the group within its wider context, and protect the workers from criticism from other team members. Where groupworkers are leaving the agency, and this applies especially to students, a supervisor may offer the possibilty of continuity within the agency. The supervisor may help to ensure that the agency is aware of changing needs, is in touch with members' views and circumstances, and remains flexible and responsive.

6. *Professional development*: My experience has been that social workers under-emphasise their skills both generally and in leading groups. They carry a high level of responsibility and face escalating demands, such that it is not uncommon for social workers to feel under siege, overburdened and exhausted. Supervision has a symbolic value since it represents a commitment to professional development and growth. It has a pragmatic purpose too. A supervisor may enable practitioners to develop their skills and knowledge by helping them to specify what knowledge, experience and feelings they are bringing to each task and what skills they

may transfer from other settings to the group. It offers a means for enabling them to use their abilities and develop their potential to the full and to assess their own performance.

To summarise, supervision provides an opportunity to discuss and share responsibility for the group. It is a means of support and a sounding board for ideas. It offers a chance to share experiences, insights and problems and to draw on the experience of others. A supervisor is someone who can help resolve difficulties between the co-workers, who can facilitate the process of the co-work relationship and of the group, who can keep each on course and help the group-workers consider what action to take, when and how. It provides an opportunity to clarify areas of difficulty, to anticipate likely problems and to plan responses. Finally, the use of a supervisor is one way of acknowledging and using the interests and experiences of other team members. Their knowledge may prove freeing in the sense that it allows groupworkers to abandon the notion that they must possess all the skills necessary for effective groupwork.

Choice of supervisor

In many agencies there is an absence of choice. One person is allocated the task of supervision. I would argue strongly in favour of choice or at least for some preparation prior to embarking on a supervisory relationship. My rationale for this view is that there is no guarantee that a supervisory relationship will meet the needs of practitioners productively. As West has illustrated (1981;1982), there are important variables in any supervisory relationship. Some social workers learn inductively, through doing followed by theorising; others learn deductively, theorising before doing. Some practitioners work intuitively, others cognitively. Some groupworkers are basically extrovert, others introvert. Counter-productive difficulties may emerge, for example in problems of communication, when these functional differences are not acknowledged. Considering these variables

activities and to ensure that the work is consistent with
the goals and expectations of the agency or is their role
that of imparting their knowledge, expertise and skills? In
other words, does the supervisor's position within the
agency mean that they are accountable for the leaders'
work? This is even more relevant when the co-workers
are members of different teams or organisations. Here
the limits to the authority of the supervisor need to be
clearly delineated and decisions made concerning the
amount of reporting back to these teams or agencies.

4. Do the co-workers know the supervisor equally well?
   Where the supervisor of one of the co-workers is to
   supervise the partnership, it is important to pay some
   attention to the change in roles and to devote some time
   to becoming acquainted. The use of personal profiles may
   prove helpful here, both to provide personal details and
   to enable the participants to see what is available within
   the relationship.

5. What do the co-workers want from supervision? What
   roles are they looking for from the supervisor? What
   roles does the supervisor feel comfortable with? It may be
   helpful at this stage for supervisors to share with the
   groupworkers their assessment of their strengths, weaknesses and skills and for the co-workers to provide potential supervisors with a job description and some details
   about the proposed group, the stage of the co-work
   relationship, and their confidence as individuals. This will
   provide the basis for ensuring that roles are clear. If the
   purpose is clear, supervisors should know whether they
   possess the knowledge and expertise to help the groupworkers practise effectively. If it is unclear, there is an
   increased likelihood that expectations will be disappointed and that difficulties or important issues will be
   neglected.

6. Do the supervisor and leaders share a rationale about
   groupwork and a theoretical framework? Discongruent
   theoretical models can inhibit the usefulness of the supervisory process. Participants should share some common
   ground about group processes and theoretical concepts.
   Otherwise it is likely that different models and languages

will lead to frustrated communication and to a failure to bring practice and theory together. Additionally, there must exist at least the potential for basic trust if supervision is to meet the demands and issues inherent in groupwork practice. This trust will be fostered if the participants share similar approaches to learning and practice and if agreement is established concerning the extent to which supervision is to focus on group dynamics, the co-work relationship, groupwork techniques or wider issues of the systems with which the group is interacting.

7. Just as co-work partnerships and groups pass through a variety of stages, so too a supervisory relationship. Broadly, the relationship will be marked by phases of coming together, embarking on the task, revision and redefinition of the task and the relationship, further focus on the redefined task, and maturation. The most important phase when considering the relationship at the outset is that of revision. It is essential to build the concept of revision into the structure of the relationship, to set time aside for considering the extent to which supervision is meeting the groupworkers' needs. This may help the participants to raise areas of dissatisfaction and thereby enable the process to be more productive.

Once these negotiations have been concluded, I suggest that the decisions are recorded in the form of a written contract. This should set out clearly the structure, frequency and purpose of the meetings and the roles which the supervisor is to adopt.

The focus and content of supervision

In this discussion of supervision a model has been presented of an individual supervisor. This is not intended to preclude other models like group supervision where several co-working partnerships meet with one or more supervisors. Rather, the foci, content and guidelines for establishing supervision are similar whatever the model.

The focus and content of supervision will be detemined by the phase which the groupworkers and group have reached. Co-work terminology will be employed for these stages. However, individual practitioners will be able to locate themselves and their tasks within this framework. For them stage one is marked by self-preparation. Stage two involves preparation to work with the group and developing themselves as groupworkers. Issues relating to leading the group and maintaining themselves as resource figures occur in the third stage whilst self-evaluation and termination of the group form the final phase.

Inevitably, in deciding the agenda for supervision, practitioners will face the question of priorities, especially the choice between breadth and depth. This is a matter for negotiation. The intention of this book is to highlight points which may need to be considered. Leaders may find it easier to raise issues relating to the group rather than those relating to the co-work relationship. Perhaps this is because the former are more accessible and less threatening. However, the effectiveness of groupwork depends on the viability of the co-work partnership and, accordingly, this should be thoroughly discussed in supervision. Since an infinite number of situations can arise in the course of planning and running a group, it is helpful if the supervisor knows in advance what the co-workers wish to discuss and has a written summary either of the group or of the co-workers' preparatory discussions. This will help the supervisor to tune into the workers.

Stage One: Formation and preparation of the co-work relationship

The focus and content of supervision here is threefold. First, organisational issues relating to the group. Where the proposed group is only a blueprint, the supervisor may assist the co-workers in formulating a proposal through the use of simulation exercises and discussion. The supervisor can present a profile of the demands and problem situations presented to the agency and encourage the groupworkers to prioritise client groups in order of preference for working with them. This will establish whether there is a compatibility of interests between co-workers and between them and the agency. This may be followed by describing the situation as perceived by the agency and encouraging the groupworkers to formulate proposals for a group. The supervisor is a resource figure at this point, possessing knowledge about the agency and the demands the particular client group presents to it. The task is to share in devising a basic framework which focusses on:

- the general interests and areas of work which practitioners are seeking for experience;
- specifying the purpose of the group, ensuring that aims are realistic;
- deciding the type of group and the methods to be used;
- specifying the theoretical bases from which practitioners work.

Questions of obtaining referrals, membership selection, length of group and frequency of meetings come later. Here the need is to devise possible aims and objectives for the group. From these deliberations the participants will be able to assess the knowledge and experience they are bringing to the task and whether this needs to be supplemented by direct teaching from the supervisor or by further reading.

Secondly, individual issues which otherwise may impede the workers' development individually or of the co-work relationship. The task for the supervisor is to enable the workers to:

- relate past experiences to the present task;
- consider how their styles and value-base might influence their approach to and goals for the group;
- discuss expectations about co-working, groupwork and supervision;
- identify personal and professional strengths so that these might be available for the group;
- identify what the practitioner knows, feels and has experienced within groups.

Knowledge may include teaching received and acquired theoretical frameworks. Feeling may involve articulating fears, fantasies and assumptions which need to be shared in order to release creative work. Many groupworkers feel that their groupwork skills are limited and that they lack confidence. Their practice can be facilitated through making explicit their skills and resources and the knowledge they have gained from membership of many different groups.

Thirdly, interpersonal issues confronting co-workers. Each practitioner will have ideas about the strengths, hopes, fears, advantages and difficulties of the proposed pairing. Practitioners may find it easier to discuss the positives, what the relationship offers them and the group, and the supervisor may have to encourage the groupworkers to express any personal anxieties or early problems encountered by the pairing. Co-workers may be reluctant to mention anything about each other which they find irritating in order not to risk a rift in a valued relationship. Other concerns might be that such disclosure would weaken the partnership of jeopardise either a student placement or the viability of the proposed group. If these concerns are raised and handled sensitively, the feared eventualities will not arise. What is important is that these difficulties, fears and disadvantages are not minimised since they have a direct bearing on the effectiveness of the co-work relationship. Equally, the positives need to be examined carefully. A supervisor can help practitioners to express their hopes, to test out whether the relationship can meet these expectations and to examine whether these positives are being emphasised in order to minimise or deny difficulties. Accordingly, the supervisor's tasks might include focussing on:

- issues or dynamics between potential co-workers which they might be overlooking;
- identifying and examining their expectations, needs and problems within the partnership;
- identifying and stressing their mutuality so that the stability of their partnership might be enhanced;
- looking for overt and hidden tensions and strengths.

Supervision should focus also on the theoretical orientation of the leaders, their manner of handling and identifying problems, and the quality and quantity of their participation since these are crucial factors in promoting successful co-working (Paulson *et al.*, 1976). As with all the tasks I have mentioned, this may be done by using the exercises I described in Chapter Five. If used in conjunction with reflection on the co-workers' use of supervision, on their own preparatory discussions and on their efforts at planning their group, the participants may arrive at an understanding of how open and trusting the co-workers are with each other and the supervisor. It will become apparent whether they compete for attention and whether there is any conflict or collusion between them. Supervision may mirror their interaction within the partnership generally, for example in who defers and who reports. Ultimately, the participants will judge whether there is a workable balance between their similarities and differences.

This may provide valuable evidence on the workings of the partnership and on the problems and difficulties which need to be resolved in order for the pairing to be effective. The supervisor is concerned with developing rapport between the co-workers. The rationale for this approach is that this emphasis on the co-work relationship in its formative stages will help to increase its effectiveness. Where the supervisor helps the leaders to overcome difficulties in their relationship, they may gain confidence in the process approach to the resolution of problems. This may prove valuable in the group. Neglect of the co-workers' relationship may make for problems for the practitioners within the group.

Stage Two: Preparing to co-work the group and developing the co-work pairing

Once again the focus and content of supervision is threefold. The organisational issues relating to the group will move on from discussing the type and aims of the group to questions of membership, referrals, frequency and duration. These can cause practitioners much concern. They may experience difficulty in planning a group which is realistic in terms of their other commitments. They may find it hard to specify for whom the group is intended or to obtain referrals. They will have to negotiate resources and a budget for their group. Selecting members may seem especially problematic, ensuring a workable balance between ages, personalities and presenting problems. Practitioners may become discouraged if the co-operation of colleagues is not forthcoming. The supervisor may be able to assist the groupworkers present their project to colleagues and to understand and cope with negative reactions or anxieties displayed by team members.

The supervisor's knowledge of the organisation may prove useful in ensuring good liaison between the groupworkers and the agency and in clarifying the following issues (Hodge, 1985):

- agency expectations concerning recording and reports;
- the amount of information to be exchanged between groupworkers and colleagues when referrals are being sought or on the termination of the group;
- whether the case worker or groupworkers hold overall responsibility for the agency's involvement with a group member;
- to whom the groupworkers are accountable, particularly when they work for different agencies or teams, and whether the respective agencies or teams accept the groupworkers' attitudes towards confidentiality and their objectives for the group. Particularly relevant is the identification of those whose authority and support is required, who need to be informed and consulted.

Prior to the beginning of the group it may be useful to consider in supervision problems which might be encountered in the group and their possible solutions, the division of roles for the groupworkers both within the group and between sessions, and how the programme for the group might be organised so as to meet its objectives.

In addition to considering issues relating to the group, some focus is necessary on the individual workers and the co-work relationship. This is because the relationship will be in its infancy and the groupworkers may not feel confident.

One task within supervision is to attempt to increase the security of each individual by mobilising the skills and knowledge which each worker possesses. This may be done by drawing out past learning and connecting skills and knowledge used in contexts outside the group. The supervisor should encourage self-expression since this may help to free groupworkers from fears concerning groups. Otherwise they might encounter problems early in the group and find their effectiveness impaired. With reference to these fears, supervision may help the workers to realise the potential within a group for control and to work out their own styles of control. This may reduce their concern about a group's hostility. Guidance and the expression of confidence by the supervisor may help workers deal with their fantasies of group disintegration. Where workers have little previous experience of leadership in groups, or where they feel uncomfortable with the scrutiny of group members, or where they find it difficult to cope with the powerful emotions which can be expressed in groups, sharing these in supervision may help to modify these problems. Throughout, the supervisor and the workers should focus on how the worker may be able to meet the likely demands of the group.

The supervisor also will need to address interpersonal issues between the co-leaders. The triad may consider together how the co-workers are working together and any interpersonal issues which are affecting their functioning as a pairing. For example, is the partnership based on feelings of personal weakness and where the workers discount themselves, or is the pairing based on mutual respect where there is an awareness and creative use of differences and where a positive interpersonal relationship is modelled for the group's members? Once again the supervisor's task is the development of rapport between the co-workers. A focus on both intra and interpersonal issues is essential if the partnership is to progress and develop the quality of its work. It offers the opportunity to develop innovatory work and to create a relaxed and stimulating partnership.

Stage Three: Co-leading the group and maintaining the co-work relationship

Taking individual issues first, supervision will concentrate on the personal development of the individual worker, on increasing their understanding of their own behaviour and personality and its effect on group members. Some focus may become appropriate on a worker's security operations, the roles adopted to cope with the group experience (Williams, 1966). If a worker experiences the need to control, to avoid self-exposure or to be liked, supervision may help the leader to understand the fears or dynamics underlying these roles and enable them to reassess the threat experienced by them and to open up within the group.

Concerning interpersonal issues, a continued focus on the co-work relationship will ensure its continued vitality and effectiveness within the group. In particular the dynamics of the group may stir up issues within the pairing, for instance of competitiveness, which will need to be dealt with if the group is to continue to be beneficial to its members.

Perhaps because it seems personally threatening or potentially damaging to the co-work relationship, some practitioners may wish not to discuss in supervision dynamics and experiences within the partnership which they are finding dissatisfying or difficult. These could include feeling that the style and personality of their colleague is inhibiting their own or that they are letting their partner down. They may have formed different views about the group or feel that they are either too similar or uneasy about expressing differences, either of which could be having a negative effect on the group. Clearly, it is easier to discuss the strengths and advantages of a pairing, such as a common understanding and method, a developing friendship and congenial styles. The supervisor will need to demonstrate considerable sensitivity and to construct a safe environment for the expression of the dissatisfying aspects of the relationship which, if left unresolved, may reduce the effectiveness of the co-workers in the group. Useful questions to ask here include:

– how well are the co-workers working together?

- what do they see as the difficulties and strengths in the pairing?
- what have been their best and worst experiences in the group?
- what are their feelings towards each other?
- what do they feel to be satisfying and dissatisfying aspects of their pairing?

If the co-work relationship is proceeding smoothly, the main focus for supervision will be the group. I disagree strongly with statements that supervision is less important in this phase (Dick *et al.*, 1980). Certainly, co-workers may be able to monitor their own and each other's performance but I see this as supplementing rather than replacing supervision.

Clearly, what is discussed will be influenced by the group's purposes. The following may be useful pointers however:

- how is the group progressing towards achieving its aims? What developments in the group are contributing towards this progression and what are impeding it? What part are the co-workers playing in these developments?
- what is the group's programme and how does this relate to the group's aims?
- is any revision of the group's aims or length necessary?
- what particular problems have arisen in the group between members or between leaders and members? How might these be dealt with?
- what theoretical frameworks help to make sense of the group's development and dynamics? How might these be incorporated into the groupworkers' practice within the group?
- are the styles of the leaders facilitating the group? Are the co-workers participating equally or are their feelings towards the group, the members or each other impeding their interaction with the group? Is their behaviour in the group congruent with their feelings and the group's process?

Quite simply, the emphasis is on increasing the practitioners' awareness of the group's process and on developing their interpersonal skills and professional expertise. The supervisor may achieve this by offering constructive criticism and praise, by encouraging self-criticism and evaluation and by reassuring workers of the universality of the experience of understanding one's activity without necessarily feeling able to control it.

Stage Four: Evaluation and termination of the group and co-work relationship

Much evaluation takes place within supervision (Preston-Shoot, 1985). The supervisor's role will depend on the confidence and skills of the practitioners in this field. However, they can assist the workers to evaluate the outcome of the group and their partnership, to identify and incorporate what they have learned and to communicate their views to their colleagues. They may help them to identify their feelings related to the loss of the group and close working relationship with a colleague, and to specify appropriate next steps for group members and the leaders.

Conclusion

Supervision is not an easy undertaking. It requires commitment, sensitivity and perseverance, especially when the supervisor perceives issues which need to be tackled but which the leaders are avoiding. There are also the questions of assessment and evaluation which loom large for students but probably are crucial to all workers and essential for further development. From this discussion it will be apparent that supervisors need to possess a variety of skills. They may find it necessary to be an advocate, to present the view of the groupworkers to other staff members or agencies. They may have to be directive or find themselves in the role of a specialist, providing knowledge in a particular area of work. Supervision may involve collaboration in problem solving and providing suggestions concerning alternative approaches to problems, issues and aims. Alternatively, supervisors might need to comment on the processes within the group or co-work relationship, concentrating on communication between the workers and between them and the group. This may involve identifying and exploring themes and underlying topics, for instance anger towards one group member or conflict between the practitioners which is revealed in their discussions within supervision. Finally, the supervisor's style might be non-directive, facilitating the practitioners to identify themes and problems and to work on finding solutions for themselves.

Supervisors should be careful not to stunt the spontaneity of the workers by making them too self-conscious or by offering too many comments of what they would have done (Yalom, 1970). Suggestions can be turned all too easily into a doctrine of perfection where the supervisor's approach becomes the way to lead a group. The supervisor should be careful not to favour one of the workers or to allocate one to the role of senior unless this is an explicit division within the co-work relationship. Finally, to increase the possibility of transferring knowledge and skills from one context to another, the supervisor should link explicitly the practitioners' practice in this group with their experience in social work generally and in working with other groups. When supervisors feel comfortable with this variety of roles and when practitioners feel congenial with their supervisor, the process can be very useful. Indeed, working with groups is inadvisable when supervision is not available.

8

Evaluation

Introduction

This chapter has two purposes. First, to indicate the value and scope of evaluation. Secondly, to convey a sense of its feasibility by describing how practitioners might use an evaluative approach in their groupwork practice.

It has never been professionally desirable or ethically acceptable simply to appeal to a value-base or to rely on banner headlines to justify service provision. Moreover, it is becoming increasingly difficult to rely on assumptions that services help people or that groupwork is a 'good thing'. In the current climate of economic constraints, it is no longer acceptable to be unclear how groups help people, in what circumstances and for how long. Practitioners cannot remain unresponsive to those who demand evidence and whose verdict is that social work is at best unproven and at worst ineffective. Social workers have a responsibility to specify what they can do and how, to adopt a consciously evaluative attitude to their work.

However, Sheldon (1982) believes that very little evaluation of practice is undertaken. My research suggests that practitioners appreciate their professional responsibility to evaluate their work but doubt the adequacy of their tools and are bewildered by the complexity of the processes and problems to be evaluated (Preston-Shoot, 1985). They acknowledge that evaluation helps to define areas of achievement or further work and provides feedback on progress. However, although it provides an assessment of whether their methods have been effective, practitioners experience difficulty in establishing and developing a consistent pattern of evaluation. This seems to be because they are unclear about the methods to use and, confronted by a range of interwoven problems, are uncertain about whether it is possible to disentangle them and define categories on which to concentrate.

This situation has arisen for a number of reasons. First, evaluation is seen as requiring different skills from social work intervention. This chapter will show that evaluation skills and techniques have much in common with social work practice generally. Secondly, evaluation feels threatening and produces anxiety, perhaps because it is defined in terms of success and failure rather than as contributing to a group's development and to a worker's practice, which seems to be a more correct judgement. Thirdly, concern is expressed about the possible negative effect on workers and consumers of not achieving specified objectives. Allied to this is the concern that undue stress on evaluation will alter the group's atmosphere and divert energy from service provision. Practitioners are often worried that the complexity and richness of the groupwork experience will be lost and that groups will be organised around considerations of evaluation alone. However, the setting of clear, realistic goals and the monitoring of progress improves effectiveness and enhances rather than detracts from groupwork. Moreover, it enables consumers to experience the satisfaction of achievement. Indeed the experience of sharing in the measurement of progress towards clearly defined objectives can be therapeutic, highly rewarding and motivating for clients. Finally, evaluation is complex. It does seem difficult to specify the effect of intervention and the degree of change or to isolate the effects of variables such as clients' self-esteem or practitioners' style and techniques. It can prove difficult to disentangle the relationship between intervention and extraneous factors on outcomes or to find unequivocal and objective criteria to do justice to the complex problems to be examined. Therefore, it is not surprising that it seems easier to describe a course of events than to evaluate whether and how aims have been achieved or which interventions or other factors have promoted change. However, models and methods are available with which to tackle these problems.

None the less, the outcome of these factors is that social workers remain relatively ill-informed about what approaches work and for whom, about who they can help and how. Therefore, it remains difficult to use experience as feedback to inform future practice.

Why evaluate?

Described above are the benefits which an evaluative approach can bring to consumers. In addition, both groupwork and groupworkers can benefit from this approach. Evaluation can improve the quality of services by ensuring that planning and activities are directed towards purposeful outcomes. It can improve the development and refinement of effective ways of helping by defining what contributes to effectiveness through producing results in an accurate and communicable form: material available for use by future workers and consumers.

Groupwork contains many variables. There are the groupworkers' skills, strengths and weaknesses, together with their leadership style and qualities such as empathy and warmth. There is the nature and degree of members' difficulties, their social situations and the extent to which they accept the rationale of the group. Then there is the quality of relationships established in the group. Giving thought to these many variables, analysing their development in and effect on the outcome of the group may help to highlight those qualities which are necessary, if not sufficient, for successful groupwork. For example, it appears that practitioners' personal, interactional style affects both outcome and how they are perceived.

Evaluation may prevent vagueness and loss of direction. At the outset, planning work with specific goals brings clarity to complicated situations where practitioners otherwise might feel overwhelmed. Equally, by referring back to and reviewing initial purposes through collecting information on the group's development, practitioners can establish important features which have occurred, why and to what extent aims have been achieved. They can establish whether further areas of work exist and whether modifications to the group's goals are necessary. That is, evaluation may offer grounds for continuing groupwork or for ending positively and appropriately rather than allowing the work to drift. Finally, evaluation on terminating work may help to define the basic necessary skills required for effective groupwork. In giving definition to core skills, evaluation adds substance to otherwise anecdotal accounts and clarifies where an intervention is especially effective in helping to achieve change. Follow-up can develop this by providing information on whether changes perceived in group members are sustained and carried over into other settings.

Results can inform practice decisions. They may suggest selection criteria for future groups and optimum time-scales for particular problems to be tackled or aims to be achieved. They may inform recommendations for further programme activity when the leaders consider their future work or provide practitioners with increased confidence and certainty in practice by indentifying their strengths and achievements. All this has considerable practice relevance.

Evaluating co-work relationships and individual practice

This is easy to overlook. Frequently, practitioners neglect how far and why their original hopes have materialised, whether and what they have learned. They overlook the effect of the group and groupwork practice on them and the impact or development of their styles of work and contributions in the group. This may stem from uncertainty about how to evaluate personal contributions and development and from not considering evaluation of individuals' practice or of co-work partnerships at the outset of the group.

This represents a missed opportunity. Social workers are a valuable resource whose resources, what they know, feel about and have experienced in groups, should be recognised and developed. Co-work is used frequently as a training modality for groupwork but how effective is it? Practitioners enter groupwork and co-work or solo leadership with a variety of hopes, aims and fears. The fears usually prove to be unfounded and the hopes realised. However, much could be learned from knowing how and why these outcomes occurred. Dowling (1979) found that practitioners frequently perceive inaccurately their own and their co-worker's behaviour. She suggests that leaders should strive for accuracy by practising recognising and categorising their interventions. The more accurately workers perceive their own behaviour, the more reliable their observations of others should be. Therefore, evaluation may help groupworkers to define varieties of roles and interventions and, thereby, contribute to clarity about what they are doing. The suggested benefit of this approach is that it provides a means of assessment and training to imrpove practitioners' efficiency and effectiveness.

To illuminate a co-work relationship or solo leader's practice beyond impressionistic assessment and description, the following procedure is suggested. At the outset, practitioners should define their starting position and their personal goals. Thus:

- what skills and knowledge do they bring to their practice?
- what do they see as their strengths in groupwork and in social work practice?
- what roles or styles of work come easily to them?
- what do they hope to contribute to this group/co-work partnership?
- in what areas do they wish to improve their practice?
- what do they find difficult in groups?
- what are they hoping to learn from co-work/solo leadership?
- what do they expect from co-work/solo leadership?
- what do they expect from a co-worker?
- what are their expectations about groupwork and leading a group?
- what developments in their practice do they hope will have occurred by the end of the group?
- what goals have they set themselves or for the co-work relationship?

Next, define indicators, pointers by which to judge the extent to which their goals have been achieved or are being approached. For example, if a practitioner wishes to develop skills in summarising what members hope a group may achieve and reframing their statements into possible goals which could be pursued by the group, the task is to identify what types of behaviour in or interaction with the group would constitute movement towards or attainment of this skill. A similar approach may be used with a wish to overcome anxiety in groups or to develop the co-work partnership.

Finally, decide what methods of collecting information will be used. Feedback from group members, including questionnaires, rating scales and interviews, may be used. Sentence completion, discussion, self-reports and self-rating scales can provide practitioners with information with which to assess progress towards their original objectives. At the conclusion of the group, therefore, leaders should be able to specify:

- which of their aims and objectives were attained.
- what they have learned.
- members' views about their practice.
- particular problems they encountered in groupworking.
- the outcome of their hopes and fears which they brought to the group/co-working.
- the extent to which, why and how their experience of co-work/solo leadership/groupwork was different from initial expectations.
- what facilitated or impeded their performance in the group.
- what facilitated or impeded their learning in the group.
- their impact on the group/co-worker.
- the outcome of their expectations of their co-worker: an appreciation of the partnership.
- further ways in which they hope to develop their skills.

This approach will enable practitioners to specify what they have learned and achieved, what they may incorporate into their future practice and whether, in co-work, the partner-ship is sufficiently congenial to use again.

Evaluation of a group

Evaluation seems to convey the impression of a postscript, a retrospective look. Ideally, however, it is an approach to incorporate into the structure of groupwork from the outset. It is an integral part of the groupwork process. Most activity which might be termed evaluation should be completed before the group's final session.

Several guidelines may assist groupworkers with evalua-tion. First, right beginnings are vital. Evaluation is on-going, not an ingredient at the close of the group. If evaluation is viewed as something which comes at the end of intervention, much potential material will have been missed or lost and there may be pressures to take on new work. In such circumstances time may present difficulties and evaluation may appear an unwelcome further task. This problem might be overcome if evaluation is incorporated into the task from the beginning.

Secondly, global aims or goals are difficult to analyse. Therefore, these concepts should be translated into specific components. For example, self-esteem can be measured but only when conceptualised precisely and reduced to its be-havioural, cognitive and emotional elements (Jones, 1985). Similarly, support needs to be defined more precisely and then evaluated by workers and members. Evaluation of very wide issues can produce only limited results. It is not that the results are unobtainable but that the questions asked are too broad or too simple. The guideline is to be specific rather than general.

Thirdly, success is one such global concept to be reframed into clearly defined elements which lend themselves more readily to measurement and specific meaning. Thus, consen-sus is required on the purposes and goals of the group. This achieved, the next step is to devise criteria with the group which will show the extent of its movement towards its objectives.

Fourthly, to think in terms of subjectivity and objectivity is unhelpful. A systematic approach should not be confused with a search for methodological perfection. Striving for objectivity is as likely to be inadequate or frustrating as vague description. Evaluation is not simply about scientific measurement but includes the workers' critical judgement and professional opinion. Rather, evaluation may be seen on a continuum from precise measurement to impressionistic enquiry, assessment and description. Therefore, groupworkers need to be clear about what evaluation they want to do, what they understand by it generally and for a particular group, what they are looking for and the methods they are to use.

Fifthly, evaluation has little value unless built into and informing policy thinking and practice. Evaluation contributes to a body of knowledge which, if utilised, may shape the structure of future practice by providing knowledge beforehand which will help to make the work more purposeful.

Sixthly, it is advisable to use more than one data source and technique for collecting information in order to correct possible bias. A worker's theoretical orientation may lead them to collect data to support their assumptions. Not only do workers need to be flexible enough to disregard assumptions when they are not substantiated but different data sources may help them to challenge their assumptions. Allied to this, for a wide-ranging assessment, systems external to the group should be included in the evaluation process. The perceptions of significant others such as caseworkers, parents and teachers can give authenticity to gains which groupworkers and members believe have been made in the group.

Finally, who is the evaluation for and what is it attempting to show? It may be designed to denote outcome or to chart progression from one point towards another without attempting to isolate the factors involved in that progression. Alternatively, it may be designed to explain the progression between these points. This will involve a detailed examination of:

- content: what was contained within group sessions.
- process: how the group was offered and received; devel-

opments in the group; what facilitated or impeded change.
- structure: the resources provided or available in the group's members; whether these were sufficient for the group's aims.
- outcome: changes in the target of the group, whether members and/or others.
- impact: changes in the target group and their environment.
- ethics: was it a proper intervention to have engaged in?
- purpose: was it likely to have achieved its goals? Was it based on sound propositions with evidence to support them?
- efficiency: are other approaches more economical? What are the advantages of this approach?
- quantification: using rating scales and other measures to express the differences and communicate about them.
- utility: will the information be used? How? (Jones, 1985).

It will involve an examination of the inter-relationship between the independent variable: the conditions in which the clients' problems exist; the dependent variable: the problem or need to be tackled; the intervening variable: methods of tackling the problems; and outcome: the result.

An evaluative approach in groupwork

How to construct an evaluative approach will depend to some extent on the group's purposes. However, general points may be made in respect of the four phases of a group at which evaluation should be considered explicitly. It is here that the core skills common to evaluation and social work intervention will be shown.

Before the first session

Groupworkers begin by devising a group in response to existing information or concerns in the agency. This involves assessment skills: getting to know the problems and how they are perceived and understood by referrers and potential members. To this is added the groupworkers' own hypotheses and formulations about the nature of the problems. Through a process of negotiation with referrers, potential members and significant others, a baseline is established: the present level of the problems; their effect, frequency and ramifications. General aims for the group are compiled, a statement of purposes and objectives. The existing information and possible aims may suggest particular selection criteria. The exact criteria will depend on the type and purpose of the group. For instance, a willingness to explore feelings or stable relationships outside the group are probably important in a discussion group. High motivation or its potential development do seem crucial, as is the extent to which prospective members share the rationale of the group. These will need to be assessed during the phases of offering the group and its initial meetings.

Once hypotheses about the nature of the problems have been framed and shared with those involved, the task is to phrase:

- the ideal result aimed for.
- targets for the group and its members.
- specific objectives and tasks informed by the group's general aims.
- a programme and intervention consistent with the above to attain the group's and members' goals.
- an estimate of the time required.
- indicators with which to judge progress towards objectives.
- data collection methods and who will collect information and when.

The aims agreed with members must be clear, specific and achievable for they form the baseline for comparison during and after the group. After the group's early meetings, everyone should be clear about the changes to be sought, how they are to be achieved, the methods thought essential and the means by which information is to be collected. Regular reviews should be incorporated into the programme and a recording system devised which will keep the group's aims in focus and lend itself to evaluation later.

The goals of members and workers do not have to be similar. However, whether there are similarities or differences, they should be written into a contract, an agreement about the specific aims and goals and about where members are starting from and the hoped-for outcome. Where there are differences, these may be incorporated into either:

- a preliminary contract: an agreement to survey what is being offered without commitment and to clarify expectations;
- or an interim agreement: a trial period either because the aims are not agreed or to establish whether the services offered are appropriate to the needs defined;
- or a reciprocal contract in which leaders and members accept that their aims are not identical but agree to co-operate in helping each other achieve their different goals.

Where contracts are not mutual, specify the differences and assess whether it is possible to work together on the basis of these differences (Preston-Shoot *et al.*, 1984).

Thus, shortly after the first meeting, there should exist a clear definition of what is being tackled, what the group is trying to achieve and how, and a clear statement of the position from which the group and its members are setting out.

The process of the group

Each meeting should be recorded and the content shared with members. This helps to focus the group and provides a structured opportunity to evaluate individual and group progression towards the stated objectives. The stages, purposes and goals of the group will influence the structure and content of the records. Leaders should consider what to note and how. The following may be useful to record:

- changes and developments in individuals and the group. What has been achieved and what has influenced these developments?
- the impact of the group and leaders on members.
- feedback from members.

- when and how aims were changed.
- new objectives and review dates.
- observations on whether the goals and methods are clear and how much is accomplished quantitively and qualitatively.
- whether members work together and are involved, who participates and how, and whether the group is united or divided.
- the leaders' experience of the group.
- members' response to each other and the leaders. Are they hostile, supportive, co-operative or competitive?
- how members negotiate the beginning of the group.
- the degree of trust, intimacy, involvement or conflict in the group.
- which aspects of the co-work relationship or leaders' interventions appear helpful? What happens after the workers intervene? How is the intervention perceived and used? What is its impact?
- which parts of the group's structure or programme appear helpful?

Diagrams may prove useful to illustrate who talks to whom and who contributes. Questionnaires may enable members to make suggestions or to comment on whether their expectations of the group differ from their experience. Involving members in recording enables the workers to check the accuracy of their observations and some comparison to be made between the members' and leaders' views of what has occurred in the group and what needs to be changed or done. Interviewing significant others may be helpful when leaders wish to know whether changes observed in the group are to be found also outside it, or to correct any desire to please which members may feel to avoid the cognitive dissonance of denying benefit from a group established to help them.

Termination

Here the group should re-examine the original objectives and weekly records to assess:

- what has been achieved, to what degree and what may explain this.
- the effectiveness of the methods and leadership styles used.
- whether the group has made a difference to members, with evidence to support the view presented.
- unintended consequences of the group.
- the influence of factors within and external to the group. Evaluation should not focus exclusively on individual members or the group in isolation from the agency in which it functions and the members' external circumstances.
- what clients expected the group to be like and whether and in what ways the group was different from what members expected.
- any suggestions clients may have about the time, place, length of sessions and the group's content.
- from the outcome of the group, what may be incorporated into future groupwork. What have the leaders learned from being with this group?

This data may illuminate the appropriateness of concluding the group and how members may continue to work on their goals after the group. It may demonstrate too the advantages and drawbacks of the type of group or format adopted, or highlight resource, agency and organisational issues which can be used to inform future groupwork planning and service provision for individual members. By this stage, therefore, a clear statement should be available of what happened together with some hypotheses as to why.

Follow-up

This is very important but often neglected: important in determining how long the benefits derived from the group have endured and the extent to which members have found the group experience valuable or useful. Members' views concerning what has been helpful may change over time as gains become apparent outside the group or familiar difficulties return. Data collected in a follow-up may provide evidence to validate or question an approach which can be placed alongside the perceptions of the groupworkers.

The omission of follow-up has sometimes been explained as due to the absence of funding, workers leaving the agency, and an open-ended group. However, how useful have members who have left an open-ended group found the experience and will their views not have some relevance for the group's aims? Nor should workers leaving an agency prove an intractable problem. An independent evaluator may help to offset the difficulties of bias and of members feeling that they have to report improvements if they feel that this is expected or are embarrassed by any failure of the group to produce the desired results. Some follow-up is highly desirable where members are to be considered for future groups.

Although the exact content of follow-up interviews or questionnaires will be influenced by the group's objectives, it may be appropriate to attempt to obtain members' views on:

- the difficulties or concerns which led them to agree to membership.
- the degree of choice which they felt they had.
- the extent of their difficulties at the beginning and conclusion of the group and at the point of the follow-up. Rating scales may be helpful here.
- their views on why change did/did not occur and whether the group was responsible for any change.
- what they and the group attempted to do to resolve their difficulties.
- their comments on the content and relevance of the group for them.
- aspects of the group they felt important and liked.
- what they found difficult in or disliked about the group.
- whether and in what areas they feel the need for further services. Have any difficulties arisen due to the group or since its conclusion?
- any general comments about the group, any suggestions for improvements? (Sanderson, 1985).

Client participation

Explicit in the above discussion has been the direct involvement of group members. The arguments in favour of client participation are overwhelming. Professional self-respect, ethics, the evidence that many clients feel unsure about what services they can expect to receive and the requirement to be certain that groupwork is achieving its goals all point to the urgency of including clients as fellow citizens.

The value principle of consumer involvement in all stages and at all levels of the social work process has become a characteristic of the eighties. Shaw (1976) has identified four reasons for this. First, a distaste for professionalism and a reassertion of clients' abilities to diagnose their own needs or evaluate the services they receive. Secondly, disillusionment with current political representation. Thirdly, a decline of psychoanalytical concepts and fourth, research findings which have suggested that social work conveys only marginal benefits. To these add the evidence that social workers' and clients' perspectives may not coincide and often clash. Thus, what do consumers feel about groupwork? How do they appraise the services being offered? Client participation can provide much valuable and informative material.

Group members, including children, should be involved in the evaluation of a group and of a co-work relationship or a solo leader's practice. Children can react very well to the responsibility of assessing progress, of talking about the group and answering questions. This is not simply a value position in support of client participation and of a move away from seeing clients as the passive recipients of services. It has too a pragmatic purpose. Client involvement increases morale and productivity. Including members may help to increase the reality of the goals for the group and may help to commit clients and leaders to shared objectives. It encourages their participation in the group and promotes the development of self-valuing.

Of course, there are difficulties in adopting a policy of client participation. The first difficulty is deciding when client opinion has been understood. The inter-relationship between satisfaction and success or failure, between criticism and knowledge of services, and between expectations, the help received in past encounters and the characteristics of the social worker is complex. Satisfaction may be linked to lack of knowledge, limited expectations or actual helpfulness. A second difficulty is of using an understanding of client opinion in policy formation especially where groups of clients express different opinions (Shaw, 1976; 1984). A third difficulty arises from research into client opinion using social workers' frames of reference when the issues for study are defined from within social work (Phillimore, 1982). Here, detachment from the social work milieu, that is where clients are enabled to comment freely rather than within parameters set by social workers, may enable practitioners to learn more about how clients experience social work and group membership.

These difficulties are not intractable and the slowness with which social work is operationalising the philosophy of client involvement reflects an inbuilt conservatism rather than the absence of means to overcoming the difficulties described.

Methods

The method described is a goal model, measuring achievement against specific statements of aims. To be satisfactory this approach needs to be incorporated from the outset. Objectives, that is what is being aimed at, need to be clear, specific and achievable. With these in mind, indicators of change can be formulated, pointers which will tell the group whether the objectives have been or are being reached or whether revisions are necessary. Thereafter, what is required is a systematic way of collecting information. Methods of doing this are offered below.

Impressionistic enquiry is a means of subjecting information gathered by interviews, recording and observation to critical appraisal. It gives scope to the insightful, intuitive skills of the evaluator. It is an assessment of movement towards objectives and of the reasons for this, using events, relationships, interactions and behaviour in the group.

Where the group is focussing on behaviour, types of

behaviour can be listed on a checklist and ticked off or rated for each member in each session. For example, members' contributions to the group can be listed and might include whether members suggest ideas, are supportive towards each other and relaxed in the group or withdrawn. Problem behaviours or difficulties relating to social contact can be listed, for instance in an Intermediate Treatment group, where the checklist might include whether members were aggressive, submissive, co-operative or demanding of attention. How the group functions in each session can be formulated into a checklist by using such headings as cohesiveness, attention to tasks, supportive of members and exercising their own controls. As with all these methods, evidence needs to be recorded to support the judgements made.

Questionnaires, sentence completion and self-reports may be used to rate and describe what members wanted and gained from the group or what they liked, disliked, remembered and found useful or unhelpful. They may be used to focus on perceptions of whether the group has dealt with its tasks satisfactorily, partially or not at all.

The content of questionnaires and sentence completion will depend on the purposes of the group and what the leaders want to know. Especially useful, however, are members' and leaders' descriptions of or views about:

- the atmosphere of the group and whether its pace felt too slow, about right or too fast.
- how interested members felt in the group, whether and why this varied, and their view of its progress.
- members' participation in the group: were members dominant, co-operative, uninvolved, hostile or supportive and involved?
- members' attitudes to the leaders, each other and the activities of the group.
- members' attitudes to significant people outside the group.
- themselves before and after the group.

The observations of significant others, such as parents, partners and teachers, may provide data concerning whether changes noted in the group have been observed outside it. This places the group's progress within a wider perspective.

Another method is observation. Groupworkers need to be clear about what they are looking for and what is important for the purposes of the group. These observations may be described diagrammatically by using sociograms to illustrate, for example, the development of interaction in the group, who talks to whom and who makes what kind of contributions.

Rating scales may be used by members and leaders. Douglas (1976) gives some examples of the types of scales which can be used:

- the clarity of goals (from no goals to very clear goals).
- the degree of trust and openness in the group (from distrust to remarkable trust).
- the extent to which there is a sense of belonging in the group (from none to considerable).
- the use of group resources (from one or two members contributing to resources used fully).
- whether decisions are made and how many members are involved in decision making.

These scales may highlight areas where difficulties impede progress and, used over time, may enable changes and developments to be monitored. Scales may be used for members to itemise the most to the least favourable change or outcome and whether achievement was more or less than expected. Finally, scales may be used to chart a member's progress in respect of a target problem. In this instance, a baseline is required prior to intervention, the point on the scale at the beginning. Clear criteria then need to be devised for placing observations on the scale. The member should be involved in defining the points on the scale in a way which is capable of being communicated to others and carries a clear meaning.

It is advisable to use several methods together. Evaluation can be concerned with process: how the group is working; outcome: what has been achieved; and impact. Using several methods widens the field of vision and avoids the possibility of distortion or bias.

Conclusion

The objective of an evaluative approach is to identify what facilitates effective groupwork and from this to form hypotheses which can be tested in other contexts. Practitioners need to be clear about the questions they are trying to answer and why they are evaluating the group since this will help to determine the methods used and questions asked. In this chapter I have given guidelines on what evaluation is, why it is important, and on when and how to start. The results may help practitioners to identify those clients who have been helped by types of groupwork and those methods which, in certain contexts, have been found to be useful.

Bibliography

Adams, R. (1984) 'Surviving the contradictions', *Community Care*, 23 August 1984.

Barclay (1982) *The Barclay Report*.

BASW (1980) *Clients are Fellow Citizens*, British Association of Social Workers.

Bion, W. (1961) *Experiences in Groups*, Tavistock.

Bloch, S. (ed.) (1979) *An Introduction to the Psychotherapies*, Oxford University Press.

Bloch, S. (1982) *What is Psychotherapy?*, Oxford University Press.

Brandes, D. and Phillips, H. (1978) *Gamesters' Handbook*, Hutchinson.

Breslin, A. and Sturton, S. (1974) 'Groupwork in a hostel for the mentally handicapped', *Social Work Today*, 4, 23, 722–6.

Brown, A. (1977) 'Worker style in social work', *Social Work Today*, 8, 29, 13–15.

Brown, A. (1979) *Groupwork*, Heinemann.

Brown, A., Caddick, B., Gardiner, M. and Sleeman, S. (1982) 'Towards a British model of groupwork', *British Journal of Social Work*, 12, 6, 587–603.

Curnock, K. and Hardiker, P. (1979) *Towards Practice Theory*, RKP.

Davies, B. (1975) *The Use of Groups in Social Work Practice*, RKP.

Davies, M. (1984) 'Training: What we think of it now', *Social Work Today*, 15, 20, 12–17.

Dick, B., Lessler, K. and Whiteside, J. (1980) 'A developmental framework for co-therapy', *International Journal of Group Psychotherapy*, 30, 273–85.

Donnellan, P. (1981) 'Supervision in groupwork', in Martel, S. (ed.) *Supervision and Team Support*, Bedford Square Press.

Douglas, T. (1976) *Groupwork Practice*, Tavistock.

Douglas, T. (1982) 'Made to measure', *Social Work Today*, 13, 36, 7–9.

Dowling, E. (1979) 'Co-therapy: A clinical researcher's view', in Walrond-Skinner, S. (ed.) *Family and Marital Psychotherapy*, RKP.

FSU (1982) *Family Involvement in the Social Work Process*, Family Service Units.

Foulkes, S. and Anthony, E. (1973) *Group Psychotherapy*, Penguin.

Garland, J., Jones, H. and Kolodny, R. (1968) 'A model for stages of development in social work groups', in Bernstein, S. (ed.) *Explorations in Groupwork*, Boston University School of Social Work.

Heap, K. (1977) *Group Theory for Social Workers*, Pergamon Press.

Hodge, J. (1977) 'Social groupwork – rules for establishing the group', *Social Work Today*, 8, 17, 8–11.

Hodge, J. (1985) *Planning for Co-leadership: A Practice Guide for Groupworkers*, Groupvine.

Hopkins, J. (1981) 'Seeing yourself as others see you', *Social Work Today*, 12, 25, 10–13.

Jones, A. (1985) 'Evaluation in Family Service Units: Perspectives and a review', *FSU Quarterly*, 36, 1–6.

Levine, C. and Dang, J. (1979) 'The group within the group: The dilemma of co-therapy', *International Journal of Group Psychotherapy*, 29, 175–84.

McCullough, M. and Ely, P. (1968) *Social Work with Groups*, RKP.

McGee, T. and Schuman, B. (1970) 'The nature of the co-therapy relationship', *International Journal of Group Psychotherapy*, 20, 25–36.

Macarov, D. (1974) 'Client-worker agreement: Necessity, desideratum or dogma?' *Social Work Today*, 4, 24.

Maluccio, A. and Marlow, W. (1974) 'The case for contracts', *Social Work (USA)*, 10, 1, January.

Muir, L. (1978) 'An application of the unitary approach in group work', in Olsen, M. (ed.) *The Unitary Model: Its Implications for Social Work Theory and Practice*, BASW.

Mullender, A. and Ward, D. (1985) 'Towards an alternative model of social groupwork', *British Journal of Social Work*, 15, 2, 155–72.

Nurse, J. (1972) 'Retarded infants and their parents: A group for Fathers and Mothers', *British Journal of Social Work*, 2, 2, 159–74.

Parsloe, P. (1969) 'Some thoughts on social group work', *British Journal of Psychiatric Social Work*, Spring.

Parsloe, P., McCaughan, N. and McDougall, K. (eds) (1977) *Groupwork: A Guide for Teachers and Practitioners*, NISW papers, No.7.

Paulson, I., Burroughs, J. and Gelb, C. (1976) 'Co-therapy: What is the crux of the relationship?' *International Journal of Group Psychotherapy*, 26, 213–24.

Penn, P. (1982) 'Circular questioning', *Family Process*, 21, 3, 267–80.

Phillimore, P. (1982) 'Some comments on the interpretation of clienthood', *FSU Quarterly*, 26, 37–43.

Piggin, L. and Watson, A. (1979) 'The decision to co-work', *FSU Quarterly*, 19, 16–26.

Preston-Shoot, M., Corden, J. and Ennis, J. (1984) 'The making and breaking of contracts', *FSU Quarterly*, 33, 17–24.

Preston-Shoot, M. (1985) 'Report on a questionnaire survey of evaluation practice and needs in FSU', *FSU Quarterly*, 36, 14–20.

Preston-Shoot, M. (1986) 'Co-leadership in groups: Decision or drift?' in

Wedge, P. and Pritchard, C. (eds), *Proceedings of the First Annual Conference, Research Related to Practice. JUC/BASW*, BASW.

Reynolds, B. (1965) *Learning and Teaching in the Practice of Social Work*, Russell & Russell.

Sanderson, M. (1985) 'Everyone at FSU was very friendly and helpful – evaluating our work via customer feedback', *FSU Quarterly*, 36, 7–13.

Selvini, M., Boscolo, L., Cecchin, G. and Prata, G. (1980) 'Hypothesising – Circularity – Neutrality: Three guidelines for the conductor of the session', *Family Process*, 19, 1, 3–12.

Shaw, I. (1976) 'Consumer opinion and social policy: a research review', *Journal of Social Policy*, 5, 1, 19–32.

Shaw, I. (1984) 'Literature review: Consumer evaluations of the personal social services', *British Journal of Social Work*, 14, 3, 277–84.

Sheldon, B. (1982) 'A measure of success', *Social Work Today*, 13, 21, 8–11.

Sturton, S. (1972) 'Developing groupwork in a casework agency', *British Journal of Social Work*, 2, 2, 143–58.

Tuckman, B. (1965) 'Developmental sequences in small groups', *Psychological Bulletin*, 63, 384–99.

Walrond-Skinner, S. (1976) *Family Therapy: The Treatment of Natural Systems*, RKP.

Walrond-Skinner, S. (ed.) (1979) *Family and Marital Psychotherapy*, RKP.

West, J. (1981) 'Supervision and management in a student unit', in Martel, S. (ed.) *Supervision and Team Support*, Bedford Square Press.

West, J. (1982) 'Student, supervisor and personality type', *FSU Quarterly*, 27, 1–9.

Whitaker, D. (1975) 'Some conditions for effective work with groups', *British Journal of Social Work*, 5, 4, 423–39.

Whitaker, D. (1985) *Using Groups to Help People*, RKP.

Williams, J. (1982) *FSU Groupwork Research: Interim Report*, Unpublished.

Williams, M. (1966) 'Limitations, fantasies and security operations of beginning group psychotherapists', *International Journal of Group Psychotherapy*, 16, 150–62.

Yalom, I. (1970) *The Theory and Practice of Group Psychotherapy*, Basic Books.

Zaro, J., Barach, R., Nedelman, D. and Dreiblatt, I. (1977) *A Guide for Beginning Psychotherapists*, Cambridge University Press.

Index